COMING TO TERMS

A Mass Shooting Survivor's Reckoning
with Vulnerability and Self-Protection

COLDAW
PUBLISHING

COLDAW
PUBLISHING

For information, including that on quantity discounts, contact the publisher at:

COLDAW PUBLISHING
C. D. Michel
284C E Lake Mead Pkwy, Suite 530
Henderson, NV 89015-5511
admin@coldawpublishing.com
(562) 216-4457

Images Provided Courtesy Of Jason O. Crye, © BrokenSphere / Wikimedia Commons, © Famartin/ Wikimedia Commons, © Integrated Logistics Support Center (ILSC)/Wikipedia Commons, © Mike Searson/ Wikimedia Commons, McGeddon, San Francisco Chronicle/Polaris, Diana Miller Photography, David Frankel and Salvador Litvak, Windfall Pictures, Carol M. Highsmith's America, Library of Congress collection, Raxpixel Ltd

Cover Design: Jason O. Crye
Project Manager/Editing/Layout: Grace Wu
ISBN: 978-0-9884602-6-3
Library of Congress Control Number: 2019910625

Printed and bound in the United States of America
at Color House Graphics, Grand Rapids, Michigan.

CONTENTS

Foreword v

Dedication ix

Acknowledgments xv

Preface xvii

Chapter 1: Prologue 1

Chapter 2: 101 California Street 5

Chapter 3: Sealed Fate 9

Chapter 4: Lost Friends, Broken Hearts 15

Chapter 5: Channeling Grief 17

Chapter 6: Seattle Shadows 23

Chapter 7: Aloha Fear And Frustration 29

Chapter 8: Big Sky Revelation 33

Chapter 9: Black Hills Badass 37

Chapter 10: What If 41

Chapter 11: Coming To Terms 43

Chapter 12: "Do Something!" 49

Chapter 13: Epilogue 55

About The Author 59

Appendix: *District of Columbia v. Heller*
Majority Opinion 61

FOREWORD

by Chuck Michel

The terrible and tragic murders of eight people, with six more injured by a deranged gunman at the law firm of Petit & Martin in the office tower at 101 California Street in San Francisco in 1993 spurred liberal San Francisco lawyers to channel their grief into creating the association that has effectively become the law firm for the gun ban lobby. The group was initially called the Legal Community Against Violence (LCAV), later rebranded as the Law Center to Prevent Gun Violence, and then rebranded again as the Gifford's Law Center to Prevent Gun Violence (GLCPGV) (hereinafter referred to as the "Center").

This special interest group has received multi-million dollar block grants from progressive foundations and pro-bono support from large liberally inclined or social activist law firms that have their own extreme left agendas in many cases. The Center relentlessly pushes model gun bans in cities across California and the country to this day and uses every legal trick in the book and then some to accomplish its agenda.

Creative lawyers associated with LCAV first came up with an inventive and dubious legal argument to try to hold gun manufacturers and distributors legally liable for the misuse of their products by criminals, and then rallied about a dozen cities run by liberal politicians to file lawsuits against gun manufacturers, wholesalers and retailers in an effort to bankrupt the firearms industry. Although these cases ultimately meet with little success under the expansive and unconventional legal liability theories they advocated, the lawsuits inflicted tremendous financial damage on the firearms industry, which roughly makes in a year what the tobacco industry makes in a day.

The coordinated legal onslaught was mostly stopped by the passage of the NRA and National Shooting Sports Foundation (NSSF) which promoted the Protection of Lawful Commerce in Arms Act (PLCAA) in 2005. Under the PLCAA, firearm manufacturers and dealers can still be held liable for damages resulting from marketing defective products, breaching contracts, criminal actions, and other things, just as manufacturers and sellers of other consumer products can be held liable. They can also be held liable for negligent entrustment when they have reason to know a gun is intended for use in a crime. But PLCAA blocks lawsuits to hold firearms manufacturers, wholesalers, and retailers liable for the criminal misuse of their products. Efforts to repeal or get around the PLCAA continue, now largely supported by gun ban advocacy groups and lawyers funded by billionaire social engineer Michael Bloomberg.

Working with their associated public relations professionals, the Center also helped to develop the benign sounding talking points used to this day by the gun ban lobby and politicians with a civilian disarmament agenda. That's why you hear politicians speak reassuringly of their "respect" for the Second Amendment (their toothless version of it anyway) and the need for mere "common sense" gun "safety" laws, while unjustifiably demonizing whole classes of firearms with sinister sounding emotion-laden but technologically nonsensical buzz words like "assault weapon" or "Saturday Night Special." Using trained techniques, gun ban advocates have become masters not only of rhetorical manipulation, but also of using carefully crafted rhetoric to manipulate public emotion to advance their underlying gun ban policy agenda.

Many people see through this propaganda sooner or later. They come to terms with their own vulnerability, and make personal choices about how to protect themselves and their families and limit the risks to their own safety. It's an individual journey of realization, but these thinkers eventually come to realize that, in today's world, vulnerability is unavoidable. Politicians, the government, and laws cannot keep guns out of the wrong hands nor protect us from violent criminals, madmen, and terrorists. Gun control laws fail. We are not safe.

They come to realize that "common sense" gun control laws are anything but. They come to appreciate the wisdom in the maxim that "common sense is what tells us the earth is flat."

Coming to Terms is the story of lawyer David Frankel and his soul-searching journey of self-reconciliation. As a survivor of the 101 California Street shootings and supporter of the Legal Community Against Violence, David tells the story of his journey from emotion inspired ignorance and dependency born of fear, to self-reliant enlightenment and individual empowerment—all in the context of post incident traumatic stress.

Coming to Terms is an intimate, inspiring and revealing story of individual reflection, reckoning, and self-actualization from a man who lived to tell his tale, told here, so that others might not fall for the alluring deception that any government or law can truly make you safe.

C.D. "Chuck" Michel is Senior Partner at Michel & Associates, P.C., a boutique law firm located in Long Beach, California. Mr. Michel and his partners are recognized as some of the leading authorities on firearms laws. The firm has litigated hundreds of cases involving constitutional challenges to gun control laws, particularly Second Amendment challenges. Many of the firm's cases have attracted local, national and even worldwide media coverage. His book, California Gun Laws, A Guide to State and Federal Firearm Regulations, is the bible on California's gun laws.

DEDICATION

*Every July 1st, I give thanks that I am among the living
and that my life story was not cut short like those of
Brian Berger, Allen Berk, Jack Berman, Deborah Fogel,
Donald 'Mike' Merrill, Shirley Mooser, Jody Sposato,
David Sutcliffe, and John Scully.*

I knew some of these individuals.

*Each year I remember all of them on July 1st and bid them
"Rest in Peace."*

MURDERED

Brian F. Berger, 39, was a senior associate at Pettit &
Martin, experienced in complex commercial litigation.
His office was on the 34th floor where the gunman
reigned unrestricted for several minutes killing anyone
wearing a suit. Brian was my mentor when I was a summer associate and then as a new lawyer at the firm. I
knew him well. He taught me a lot. He was on track to
be one of San Francisco's top commercial litigators. He
was shot in the chest and is often listed as injured. He
had a bullet lodged near his heart too close to operate
and every day it moved closer to his aortic artery until
one day about a year after the shooting it finally found
it and Brian died. He used to refer to it as living on bor-

rowed time. He was a great person, an awesome husband and a new dad at the time. It was very heartbreaking. Rest in peace Brian.

Allen J. Berk, 52, was a partner at Pettit & Martin, experienced in labor law, especially in hard knuckle union contract negotiations. Allen was a bad ass lawyer. He was a known problem solver who was willing to stick it out in late night, cigarette smoke infused labor negotiations. He was very old school. It's hard sometimes for me to remember I am now older than he was then. He died doing what I believe he loved doing - in action defending a deposition. Rest in peace Allen.

Jack Berman, 36, was a partner with the firm Bronson, Bronson, & McKinnon who was at Pettit & Martin's offices to attend a deposition of his client Jody Sposato (who was also killed). I never met Jack. Rest in peace Jack.

Deborah Fogel, 33, was a legal secretary for the law firm of Davis Wright and Tremaine, which had offices on the 32nd floor at 101 California Street. When my group of 'survivors' on the 35th floor locked the gunman in the stairway he had already killed people on the 32nd and 33rd floors. I never met Deborah. Rest in peace Deborah.

Donald "Mike" Merrill, 48, was an employee of the Trust Company of the West, which had offices on the 32nd floor at 101 California Street. I never met Mike. Rest in peace Mike.

Shirley Mooser, 64, was a secretary at the Trust Company of the West, which had offices on the 32nd floor at 101 California Street. I never met Shirley. Rest in peace Shirley.

Jody Jones Sposato, 30, was at Pettit & Martin to attend a deposition with her attorney Jack Berman (who was also killed). I never met Jody. Rest in peace Jody.

John Scully, 28, was a lawyer with Pettit & Martin who I knew very well. He was at my wedding about a month before the shooting. We socialized outside of work and I was asked to deliver, and delivered, his eulogy. I produced a music video in his honor with the permission of his family. He died while protecting his wife from the gunman's bullets. Coincidentally, they were shot in my old office on the 33rd floor that I had moved out of a month earlier before my wedding. His wife Michelle had graduated law school and was using the firm's library to study for the bar. When the shooting broke out, John left safety to find Michelle. But the gunman saw them and hunted them down. They sought refuge in my old office and tried to block the door with file boxes but it was too late. The gunman jammed his way in and in a last ditch effort, John wrapped his body around Michelle and took the bullets. A few found their way to Michelle but she survived. John died in her arms as they said goodbye and told each other they loved each other. I know this from reading Michelle's own account at the time and not from news or other reports. It still makes me want to cry sometimes. Rest in peace John.

David Sutcliffe, 30, was a law student who was interning at 101 California Street for the summer. I never met David. Rest in peace David.

INJURED

Deanna Eaves, 33, a court reporter recording the deposition of Jody Jones Sposato. I never met Deanna. I hope she recovered and has led a happy life since the shooting.

Sharon Jones O'Roke, 35, was at Pettit & Martin for the deposition of Jody Jones Sposato (killed along with Jack Berman and Allen Berk). I never met Sharon. I hope she recovered and has led a happy life since the shooting.

Charles Ross, 42. I never met Charles. I hope he recovered and has led a happy life since the shooting.

Michelle Scully, 27. I knew Michelle at that time. Michelle and John Scully were at my wedding a month before the shooting. My wife and I socialized with John and Michelle outside work a few times. They were a really nice couple. I know that Michelle recovered and remarried and as far as I know she has led a happy life since the shooting.

Victoria Smith, 41. I never met Victoria. I hope she recovered and has led a happy life since the shooting.

This book is dedicated to everyone who has made it this far in life, to the living and their families, and to the memories of those who lost their lives unjustly and tragically and to coming to terms with all of it in a good way.

ACKNOWLEDGMENTS

by David Frankel

This book would not have been possible without the California Rifle and Pistol Association. I am also grateful for the critical editorial help from Guy Smith and Chuck Michel during the early drafts and throughout the process. Tiger Lilly Enterprises publishing consultant Penny Callmeyer also deserves special mention for her patience and help in making this book happen.

I give special thanks to Chuck Michel, one of America's pre-eminent gun rights lawyers, for devoting his entire personal and professional life to defending my rights and those of my family, well before I ever became aware of the issue or even knew he existed.

I am grateful to all the national, regional, state, and local gun rights organizations, companies, and gun, hunting and shooting clubs throughout the United States. Every bit counts in the tough pull to preserve and protect the lawful exercise of the human right to keep and bear arms.

I am also grateful for public interest organizations that work to reduce the media contagion of mass shooters - #NoNameNoFame. As a mass shooting survivor,

I am grateful for the work of those who have educated the media to avoid publicizing and/or glorifying the names of the shooters. That effort alone has been very effective and may have saved thousands of lives already. It is a great example of "Doing Something" positive and effective that does not undermine the civil and human rights of others.

I am grateful for all those who have served, fought, and died to protect and preserve my right to keep and bear arms as protected by the Second Amendment to the United States Constitution.

I am grateful for the love and support of my family and the opportunity to love and support them.

PREFACE

Anyone who has read this far, may well enjoy this book. This little book, originally written in 2015, is not about victimhood or the dead; it's about survival and the living. We updated it in 2019 with a few pictures and a couple of new chapters but did not change the pre-existing chapters to reflect the passage of time.

The Supreme Court's opinion in the *Heller v. District of Columbia* case was a persuasive turning point for me. Its reflections on the natural right to self-defense, indeed, the moral obligation to defend one's self, are a lesson for us all. The majority opinion is included in the appendix for ease of reference.

CHAPTER 1:

PROLOGUE

A MASS SHOOTING SURVIVOR'S STORY

*My journey from corporate transactional lawyer,
to mass shooting survivor, to gun control activist,
to gun rights advocate*

It's a long trip from the big, vibrant, crowded and chaotic city of San Francisco, to a tiny quiet town of just 200 people in South Dakota. And it's been a long trip for me from being a corporate transactional lawyer, to surviving an infamous mass public shooting, to helping to launch America's modern gun control legal agenda, to becoming a civil rights advocate working for gun owners' constitutional rights.

The Buddha was right—*enlightenment only comes when you have traveled the entire road.*

My journey began over twenty years ago, in 1993. I was unenlightened when I made the short jump to become a gun control activist after I survived a bloody attack by an unstable former client who murdered eight

1

people and wounded six more in the San Francisco law offices where I worked. The incident is remembered by the address of the building where it happened: 101 California Street.

Bill Clinton had just become president. He promised to pass the "Brady Bill," and to enact gun bans and other forms of gun control. Clinton's gun control proposals were welcomed in San Francisco, a town then and now steeped in hard-left ideology.

San Francisco has passed lots and lots of local gun control laws, and has even tried to ban civilian handgun possession entirely. Much of San Francisco's attitude toward gun control came directly from their former city council member / supervisor, San Francisco native Diane Feinstein. She ascended to the San Francisco mayor's office, and then to a position as a U.S. Senator, after a former police officer and elected county supervisor assassinated two politicians at San Francisco's City Hall. So while Clinton was inclined to take small incremental steps to ban guns, Senator Feinstein was much more extreme. She once publicly declared that she would confiscate all handguns from civilians if she had the power to do so. Clinton later championed Feinstein's ban on semi-automatic rifles mischaracterized as "assault weapons." So she isn't particularly fond of long guns either. San Francisco was proud.

101 California Street Building From Street Level

CHAPTER 2:

101 CALIFORNIA STREET

Operating in that San Francisco reality, high on the 33rd through 36th floors of the building at 101 California Street, were the law offices of Pettit & Martin where I worked. No one is quite certain why a deranged man, whose name shall never be mentioned by me, was driven to come there on July 1st, 1993. It had been a decade since the law firm had advised him about a real estate transaction, and there was no record of general discord. After it was all over, the police found his death letter—a common artifact left by homicidal maniacs. It was a disjointed diatribe of grievances against everything from monosodium glutamate to the Food and Drug Administration. He included lawyers in his list of grievances. It still didn't really explain why he came that day. But come he did, with several guns in a briefcase, and a list of names of lawyers he had marked for death.

He came to kill them.

I was a third-year corporate transactional attorney, negotiating contracts, drafting term sheets, and closing deals for businesses at the international commerce crossroads that is San Francisco. That July afternoon had promised to be insignificant as I dealt with petty endgame negotiations between a South American businessman and his Chinese suppliers who were closing a deal. I was killing time in the office between faxes, chatting on the phone with another attorney—all very mundane. Then an urgent knock came on my office door, followed by my co-worker Steve's panicked face lunging in.

"There's someone shooting people down on 34," he said in a uncontrolled rush that lawyers normally never display. "If I were you, I'd leave… pronto."

With that Steve vanished, becoming one of the first heroes of the 101 California Street Massacre. Like a suit-and-tie wearing Paul Revere, Steve lapped around the building's 35th floor, warning everybody in the busy office of the shooter's presence in less than three minutes. At great risk to himself, Steve helped a lot of people to disappear—to quickly make themselves invisible to the gunman, who could easily come up one floor to ours.

I grabbed my briefcase and coat and joined my co-workers as they headed for the emergency stairwell with every intention of scrambling down the stairs and out of the building, away from whoever was shooting lawyers. But a line had formed at the stairwell door. Nobody was going anywhere.

"What's the hold up? Let's go!"

"We're waiting on Ron," said one of the waiting secretaries. "He's gone down to see what's going on."

I shuddered. It is a mistake to send anyone into a shooting zone, much less a 60 year old attorney. In life threatening situations, I now know, you have a choice to flee or fight. Delaying that decision can be deadly. But Ron was a senior partner so he made the call, even though in this panicked reality his authority really meant nothing. Ron's noble goal was to make sure the stairwell was safe–that if we all escaped through it, we wouldn't meet the armed madman coming up on our way down. But sending an old, slow moving fellow—a meticulous man known to stoop and pick lint out of the carpet—was not the best tactic. As we stood waiting for Ron to come back, we may as well have been waiting for the gunman himself.

Motivated by the circumstances, however, Ron was surprisingly swift. He ran back up the stairwell shouting "He's coming! He's coming this way!"

Ron flew back through the stairwell door into the office space. Two secretaries slammed the door shut behind Ron, hoping to trap the gunman on the other side. The stairwell doors at 101 California were designed for fire safety and exiting, and couldn't be easily opened from inside the stairwell. But we all knew this was a temporary measure. The gunman knew where we were, could kick or shoot through the lock, and had chased Ron up the stairs.

We all scattered, dropping files and crates as we rushed away from the coming gunman in the stairwell.

CHAPTER 3:

SEALED FATE

One of the senior secretaries told everyone to follow her, but I got a different idea. Our office had a "hidden" file room behind a section of wall. There was nothing to indicate it was a doorway – no handles, no visible hinges. I had been surprised the first time I saw a secretary push on the wall and then disappear inside. I decided the odds of the gunman not finding me were much better if I was hiding in that secret file room, so I ran there, shoved the wall door open and slipped inside.

The door sprang shut behind me, and I immediately discovered that I was not alone. There was a data entry clerk inside, typing away, surprisingly oblivious to the fact that mass murder was occurring one floor below us, and that the murderer was coming our way.

I hurriedly looked around for a weapon, anything I could use if the gunman found his way into that hidden space. The only object that came close to a self-defense tool was a heavy antique cast iron corporate seal with

a solid grip and a sharp edge. I clutched it desperately and waited, listening intently through the door. It was eerily silent outside, except for occasional unidentifiable bumping sounds or ringing phones. I imagined every noise was the murderer heading our way.

As I stood there catching my breath, time slowed down as my thoughts sped up. I realized that I was betting my life on my hiding place, and on what was basically a paperweight. The room we were in, while discreet, was easy to force one's way into if discovered. I thought about what could happen. How things might play out. I thought about my odds of survival under the difference scenarios that ran through my head. What if the shooter found this room? Would he push the door open quickly? Would he shoot through it? Could I grab his gun? How many guns might he have? Could I bludgeon him unconscious?

I realized quickly that this little hunk of cast iron was a woefully inadequate tool against an armed madman bent on killing. We were staking our lives on wishful thinking that we would not be found.

It wasn't enough. I needed something much better to defend us with. The odds of surviving were stacked against me.

A sense of vulnerability and helplessness rolled over me. I was overwhelmed by a primal desire to survive, and in thinking about how to survive, I came to recognize the meagerness of flight, or hiding, and became acutely aware of the need to be able to not only fight, but to fight effectively enough to stop a threat quickly. That sense of ill-prepared inadequacy rocked my psyche then, and haunted me for years afterwards. But at that moment it made me focus on my options, none of which were optimal.

The heightened awareness of my situational reality caused me to act. There were three other rooms inside the hidden file room area, and one of them had a better defensive perimeter than the data entry part of the hidden file room. So we slipped into the one office that had a phone and a desk and barricaded ourselves in by stacking paper-filled file boxes against the office door, six boxes deep and five boxes tall. We figured the gunman might be able to shoot his way through the door, but the thick paper barrier would keep the door closed and would slow down, maybe even stop, incoming bullets.

Maybe.

We waited. It was eerily silent. Time crept.

We didn't know where the assassin was. We didn't know if he had come onto our floor. We didn't know where our co-workers were, or what had happened to them. We didn't even know if the police were in the building.

We used the office phone to make quick calls to our loved ones, who were already in a state of panic as news of the shootings was picked up and flashed over television and radio. We got as much information as we could, which wasn't much.

After waiting a while, I actually called the lawyer who represented the other party of the business deal we were working on before the rampage began. He worked in Los Angeles, and confirmed that the 101 California Street shooting was "all over the TV." But he couldn't tell us where the shooter was, nor whether the police were inside our building. After a time-out of some twisted sense of denial, dedication, or rank stupidity—we actually did work. He and I dispensed with faxed confirmations of agreements we had been working on, and did what business lawyers almost never do—came to final terms and closed the deal on a verbal handshake.

Then we heard a single gunshot.

It was coincidental that the office we had barricaded ourselves in was on the other side of the wall from the stairwell and the gunman, still in it. Cornered in that stairwell with police closing in, and unable to continue his psychotic mission, he shot himself in the head. It's an exit plan many mass murders choose.

We heard that shot.

Of course, we didn't know at the time that it was the last gunshot, or that it was his suicide. We found that out after what seemed like hours later, when the police called everyone out of hiding—and into a corporate killing field.

That's when I became a gun control advocate.

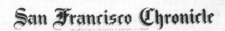

San Francisco Chronicle

FRIDAY, JULY 2, 1993

Gunman Slays 8 in Highrise

He Kills Self After Rampage at S.F. Law Office

At least 6 injured at 101 California

By James Barrett
Chronicle Staff Writer

A lone-wolf gunman stepped off an elevator and opened a downtown San Francisco highrise law office with gunfire yesterday, killing eight and wounding six before placing a 9-caliber pistol under his chin and killing himself.

Firefighters and paramedics treated shooting victims in the lobby of the 101 California building, the heavily armed assailant shot people on the 31st, 33rd and 34th floors.

Downtown Stops — 'This Is Unreal'

By Carl Nolte
Chronicle Staff Writer

OTHER STORIES ON THE SHOOTINGS

The 101 California building, with Davis Street at left

Frantic Scramble To Flee Gunman

By Dave Sneider and David Dietz
Chronicle Staff Writers

As rescue workers frantically tried to reach the people trapped in the 101 California Street building, news of the shooting spread. The tragedy was widely covered by the media.

Photo credit: San Francisco Chronicle/Polaris.

CHAPTER 4:

LOST FRIENDS, BROKEN HEARTS

L iving through the exhaustive post-massacre police debriefing was slow, meticulous, and almost as jarring as the shooting itself. As the police combed the crime scene, we learned about the people we knew and liked, the people we worked with, who had died or soon would.

There was Allen Berk, an old school style labor lawyer. Allen was tougher than ten penny nails, but also reliable and honest. He never stood a chance when he was shot like a fish in a bowl while taking a deposition at a table in a glass-walled conference room.

Allen had a better ending, if such a thing is possible, than my friend John Scully. John was chased down by the gunman on the 33rd floor. His wife Michelle was there. John died shielding her with his own body. He saved her life. It cost him his.

Brian Berger's death was the one that shook me the most. He was a friend of mine. More than a friend, he was also a mentor and an infallible guide to the

young lawyer that I was then. Although Brian was shot directly in his chest, he survived for a while. The bullet was lodged inoperably close to his heart. His doctors suspected that it would eventually kill him. Brian knew it would too, and soon. We ate lunches together after the shooting, and Brian would always say how grateful he was for his life "extension" — that he could spend a few more cherished days with his young daughter. He got several more months of life before the bullet shifted in his chest, causing some new infliction that killed him. His death hurt the most because for months I watched and spoke with this beautiful soul, a dead man who had not died yet.

Once the police released me I headed to the corner bar for the sedative that stiff drinks can provide. I called my wife to fill her in, and to calm her own nerves. A local reporter was in the bar and overheard my half of the telephone conversation. Smelling a good angle he started his interview right there, in the bar between two highball glasses.

It dawned on me that I had a story to tell.

CHAPTER 5:

CHANNELING GRIEF

When you work and socialize with people every day, you build connections. You mourn their passing. Every one of our law firm's 250 employees was hurting from our collective loss. In overt and subtle ways, surviving 101 California Street traumatized us all for years after. Our individual reactions in the aftermath of the shooting were deeply personal, often chaotic, sometimes extreme, sometimes subtle. We were all looking for answers, and desperately wanting to feel safe. It wasn't just the employees that responded. The entire San Francisco legal community was affected, and got involved in responding.

In communal grief, and shocked by trauma and sympathy, a group of San Francisco lawyers got together and created the Legal Community Against Violence (LCAV).

LCAV became the de facto law firm for the gun control lobby. Twenty plus years later, it still is.[1] There

---

[1] LCAV was renamed Law Center to Prevent Gun Violence in 2012. It was then rebranded again as the Gifford's Law Center to Prevent Gun Violence (GLCPGV)

were many sophisticated lawyers involved in starting LCAV, and they did what sophisticated lawyers do. They defined their short and long term objectives, and made plans to achieve them. Some lawyers took to the media. Local and national outlets chased the story with great intensity.

Some lawyers helped LCAV to get multi-million dollar block grants from liberal foundations to advance the LCAV's gun control agenda.

Huge sums of money were paid to a PR firm that crafted the narrative and limited the rhetoric so as not to threaten the public with talk of outright civilian disarmament. The devils in legislation are often in the details. The title of a bill often gives a distorted impression on about what the specific language of a bill actually does. So activists were taught to talk about "common sense" gun laws and to appeal to sympathy and emotion. Lobbyists were taught to be vague, to avoid getting into the details of the legislation and to "talk concept, not content" when pushing gun control bills with drafting problems, or that were intentionally drafted to actually do more than they were promoted to the public as doing.

The LCAV was very creative in its continual incremental and relentless approach to dramatically limit or eliminate gun ownership. Smart LCAV lawyers found ways of advocating the re-interpretation and expansion of existing laws so as to limit access to firearms and restrict access to the firearms culture — at gun shows for example. LCAV came up with the creative legal argument — which later resulted a landslide of expensive but unsuccessful lawsuits against the gun industry — that gun manufacturers could be held legally responsible for the criminal misuse of the firearms they sell; that Smith & Wesson, for example, could be liable for armed muggings at ATM machines. LCAV lawyers wrote persuasive memos and 'model' local ordinances that circulated around the San Francisco Bay Area, then throughout the state. LCAV caused some municipalities to enact ill-conceived gun control ordinances, and to subsequently squander taxpayer money in legal defense of those laws. These "feel good" ordinances included bans on affordable self-defense handguns (which effectively disarmed the poor), barriers to the operation of gun retailers and collectors, eliminating gun shows on city or county properties, and even in some cities trying to completely ban civilian handgun possession outright.

LCAV rapidly attracted more press attention from liberal media especially, and funding from "progressive" foundations.

I was in the middle of it all, a good gun-control soldier. I got busy. I co-produced a music video montage tribute to John Scully, the man who shielded his wife from the raging lunatic and whose eulogy I read at our firm's memorial services. I helped organize a march down California Street. I co-produced a documentary marking the first anniversary of the massacre. I never missed an opportunity to publicize our stories, especially Scully's, and to campaign for gun control. Remembering the violent trauma of that afternoon, I could see nothing but my personal grief. It obscured my rationality and perspective. Sorrow, fear, and shock motivated me, but that overwhelming emotional response clouded my logic, and that of others too.

Even as I did these time-consuming things to try and ease my grief, the panicked feeling of vulnerability haunted me relentlessly through every media event, every speech, every gun control rally that I attended. Would that cast iron corporate seal have stopped the gunman if he had discovered the hidden file room?

Would any of the laws I was advocating have stopped him?

I told myself yes. But the feeling of being trapped and helpless in that room, of irrational survivor's guilt, of vulnerability and sorrow, of the drive to do something; these all took their toll on my personal life.

There were direct and indirect costs and benefits of surviving. On the mostly positive side, I was driven to live life to the fullest—even if the approach to life was materially risky, or paid less. It was a spiritual awakening of sorts. I realized with a profound new clarity that life really was short. The cradle of a love for life is not love, or faith, or happiness. The cradle of growth for a love of life is to look straight into the face of death.

Since the massacre, I preached to everyone that they had to live their lives fully—that if they didn't wake up every day excited about what they were going to do, then they needed to change their outlook.

But I wasn't following my own gospel. My new outlook finally made me realize that big law was just an income, not a passion. San Francisco was a great city, but not a home. It was time for a change.

Some people did not appreciate my new outlook. My wife and I grew apart. Surviving, even "succeeding" day-to-day in a practical world had become unfulfilling to me. I was now indulging myself—in a full life. Is there such a thing as over-indulging in life itself? Maybe; but I couldn't slow down.

It was a big part of the reason my marriage failed.

Ultimately, I embraced a big change. A few years after the shootings I took my loyal clients, started my own law firm engineering "green tech" business deals via telecommuting throughout Canada and the United States, and left San Francisco behind.

CHAPTER 6:

SEATTLE SHADOWS

After several successful but turbulent years, I eventually wound up in Seattle with a new wife and a young child. It was a fresh start with a new perspective. But still that feeling of helplessness found its way back into my life. It was in Seattle's grittier central district that I next encountered dangerous criminals, and felt that sweeping sense of vulnerability again. One night while my wife and child slept I was awakened by the thump-thump-thump of a police helicopter and its spotlight glaring through my bedroom window. Unarmed and unsure of what to do, with that sense of exposure from 101 California Street coming back to me, I leapt out of bed and peeked out through the blinds.

Half a dozen police officers were running around shining their flashlights between our houses and into bushes, searching for a fleeing criminal in the shadows. The cops didn't have to explain their urgency. Their frantically sweeping search lights conveyed their determination, and the potential danger. They didn't need to tell me that fugitives are notoriously violent. News stories about crooks on the run breaking into homes and making hostages out of families flashed through my mind. But what frightened me most as I peered out the window was the sudden understanding that the groups of Seattle police officers running around my home and neighborhood clearly did not have the situation under control. They didn't know where the fugitive was, nor where he was headed. The police were right there, all around me, but I felt as vulnerable as I had at 101 California Street. At least in a San Francisco skyscraper danger might be contained in a stairwell or on a lower floor. Here it was running wild right in my own backyard.

I ran to the kitchen, grabbed a knife, went back to the bedroom, huddled in the dark, and waited. I watched the light from the police helicopter flare as it passed the sliding glass doors that separated our bedroom from our back yard. I stared out intently through those glass doors, desperately peering into the shadows and darkness behind my house. Nothing separated the dangerous fugitive out there from my family in here except a sheet of glass and a lock so flimsy that school boys knew how to jimmy it with a screw driver. Even an unarmed outlaw could make quick work of my family. There was nothing to stop him if he came in, except for me and my pathetic little knife.

That night I realized I was providing everything for my family—except protection. I knew that the Supreme Court had ruled that police were not legally obligated to protect us, and now the actions of the Seattle police in their frantic search confirmed that they could not provide protection for us. Hiding, cast iron paperweights, even knives weren't enough.

An epiphany. The irony of the situation was not lost on me. Here I was, a gun control activist, huddled in fear behind a glass door clutching a butcher knife and wishing I had a firearm.

The next morning I bought a shotgun.

Still being a gun control advocate, buying a gun should have been morally difficult for me. But I justified it in the name of protecting my family. I felt a twinge of guilt, of betrayal to the gun control cause, but I put away that feeling because it was painful to dwell on the deadly event that had brought me to that cause to begin with.

I bought a used pump action Remington 870 shotgun that I found at a nearby pawn shop. There was nothing special about it.

It was long, somewhat hard to manage especially in tight spaces. No finery or flash, but well-enough suited (if less than optimal) for home defense. A completely dependable piece of common hardware. And I took the precautions to learn how to use and store shotguns properly.

I didn't really mind the mandatory waiting period before I could pick up the gun—after all I had campaigned for similar "common sense" gun control measures in California.

Remington 870 Shotgun

But it now struck me as an odd precaution. I wasn't a criminal, I merely needed self-protection. And given the events of the previous night, I wanted that protection quickly. The thought of the dangerous criminal fugitive who ran through our neighborhood, and the knowledge that this waiting period didn't slow him down getting a gun, turned what I previously thought was "common sense" into an absurdity. As well-intended as the waiting-period legislation may have been, its applicability to me and millions of other threatened people who need self-defense overnight seemed misplaced. Even so, I didn't complain. I didn't protest. I didn't take equal but opposite political action to the actions I had taken supporting gun control in San Francisco. But I did realize that while I was in danger in both San Francisco and Seattle, the types of laws I once championed might be putting my new family in greater peril. I felt that something was wrong about that, but couldn't think about it clearly at that moment because I had other things on my mind.

Having that shotgun made me feel better.

CHAPTER 7:

ALOHA FEAR AND FRUSTRATION

E ven with the shotgun, the frustrating feeling of
disempowerment followed me and my family
from Seattle to Hawaii as we pursued business
opportunities. When immigrating to the Aloha State,
you have three days to register your guns. Even under
normal circumstances, this borders on cruel and unusual
punishment. When relocating to the islands, you are
wiped-out from travel on the first day. On the second
day — provided you are not frantically unpacking — you
want nothing more than a chair on the beach. On the
third day, to be in a line at the local police station, having
your fingerprints taken and being given stinkeye by the
authorities is unwelcome, inconvenient and in the case
of law abiding citizens, completely unwarranted.

I mentioned this to a friend, whose only response
was "If you don't like Hawaii's laws, move somewhere
else." A few years earlier I would have said the same
thing. But people I had known in San Francisco, law-

yers who remained there, who were working with LCAV, were working to make Hawaii's and California's extreme gun ban laws national. When restrictive laws are national, where can you move to?

The uselessness of Hawaiian gun laws became even more obvious shortly after we arrived. A neighbor's home was "invaded." In this particular type of crime, thugs enter an occupied house, typically armed with unregistered guns. Many times they just tie-up and rob the homeowners. Other times they destroy lives and wantonly murder all "witnesses." In this case they severely beat the man who lived there, then kidnapped and raped two women, locking them in the trunk of their stolen car. Those women would have died in that trunk once the daytime temperatures rose and the trunk turned into an oven. Luckily they were found in time.

Our nearby Hawaii home had even less protection than the home we had in Seattle. Fewer than 100 yards of dirt road separated our home from the street, but jungle-like vegetation obscured it well. Being low on funds from the move, we couldn't even erect a gate to keep those same thugs from driving up to our front door and doing to us whatever they pleased, whenever they pleased. And a gate wouldn't stop them anyway if they simply took the short stroll from the road.

I started noticing strangers in the neighborhood, strange cars, strange tire tracks, any sign of a threat. I was suspicious of everything. My sense of vulnerability had relocated to Hawaii with us. Even the somewhat unwieldy shotgun wasn't enough.

CHAPTER 8:

BIG SKY REVELATION

As pleasant as "green" business law was, I still felt something else nagging me professionally. I have always been a champion of civil rights, and in those days before the Supreme Court confirmed the Second Amendment and gun ownership as an individual constitutional right, I championed various causes. It was a short road for me to become a civil rights attorney, fighting mainly for people who the government was arbitrarily discriminating against. This new law practice took me many places, including Indian reservations in the Dakotas. There I helped as many individuals as I could to achieve some basic liberties long denied them. I also found time to provide pro bono assistance to an organization that helps civilians in war-torn Afghanistan and Iraq.

In 2008, I found myself far from the warm shores of Maui and working under the big skies of Montana. With seemingly endless drives between one town and the next, listening to the radio was routine. It was during one such drive that news of the *Heller v. District of Columbia* Supreme Court decision affirming that the Second

Amendment guaranteed a fundamental individual right to keep and bear arms came over the airwaves. It was a life-changing moment. Prior to that moment, I had not given serious thought to the basic issue of gun rights as civil rights. Odd as it now seems, the uncomplicated language of the Second Amendment had in my mind, and largely due to my San Francisco experience, been clouded with the narrative pushed by groups like the LCAV. Despite the Supreme Court confirmation of the individual right to bear arms both in the *Heller* decision in 2008 and in the *McDonald* decision in 2010, the LCAV still claims that the *Heller* decision "created a radical shift in the meaning of the Second Amendment," and that the Second Amendment protects almost nothing.

My dashboard radio told the *Heller* Supreme Court case story—that you, me and all our non-criminal neighbors had a right to keep arms and to defend ourselves. The statement was unambiguous and the right firmly confirmed. Yet there I was, a practicing civil rights attorney and someone who had seen both the dangers and benefits of firearms, but one who had not taken the Second Amendment of the Bill of Rights seriously. My internal philosophical conflict was as basic as the event in Seattle, when I realized that a fleeing felon had been near my back door and that my previous calls for gun control were interfering with my ability, and my right, to defend my family.

As if the radio was listening to my thoughts, it broadcast the voice of Montana's governor who said "In Montana, 'gun control' means hitting your target."

It was a long drive down Interstate 90 from Montana to Seattle and it gave me plenty of time to think.

Having just confronted my own hypocrisy over this one civil right, having just months earlier been instructed on how to handle a pistol, and knowing that, wherever I lived, I had to be the source of protection for my family, I made some decisions.

I would walk-away forever from the lawyers' gun control faction that I helped create.

I would buy a pistol, and I would get a license to carry my handgun in public.

*The type of handgun I bought after my Big Sky revelation.
I made sure to also obtain a license to carry it in public.*

CHAPTER 9:

BLACK HILLS BADASS

It is a long road to anywhere in South Dakota, and while working on civil rights issues for the natives in that state I found myself in interesting and isolated areas. Being able to defend your home is one obvious aspect of our right to bear arms. Protecting yourself on the streets and in parking lots is part of the same right, and even more important since most violent crimes occur in public. I never needed to use that Remington 870 shotgun I bought in Seattle to defend my home. But thanks to South Dakota's libertarian concealed carry laws, one night I did use a handgun I had acquired and carried with me.

Dakota Indian reservations are often vast and empty. One night I was in the middle of nowhere, meeting with a group of Native Americans who had a legal gripe with the federal government. In that corner of America and for the Lakota people, Uncle Sam perpetrated what courts call "ripe, rank and dishonorable dealings." My group of clients and potential clients and I had a long and tiring conversation that night about federal Indian law and how we might take their cases to court.

One of the potential plaintiffs was more animated and agitated about his "victimization" then the others.

Each of us may encounter someone who seems to be mentally askew, and its inevitable when screening large groups of potential clients. Some feel particularly adamant to the point of frenzy that they have a huge legal claim against the federal government. In nearly all circumstances those individuals are harmless. This unkempt fellow wasn't, as I discovered when he followed me out of the meeting hall and into the big, dark dirt parking lot. At first he merely railed about injustice, then asked for some sort of a donation, and then tried to sell me something. Then he became increasingly aggressive. His body language changed, and he started outright threatening me.

Knowing the law as it relates to confrontation and resistance, I decided to use words first. "Hey, please give me some space, you are really crowding me." He followed me anyway, getting physically closer as I reached my car. "Hey, you want me to be your lawyer, right? For free? How about you give me some space when I ask for it?" Those words triggered something in him. "You're not my f***ing lawyer!" he shouted. "Well, that suits me fine," I replied, jabbing my keys into the driver-side door of my car. "Don't give me this tough act," he said right before lunging to grab my face.

San Francisco corporate lawyers are not known for martial arts expertise, but I had taken some classes there to keep in shape. What I had learned kicked in. All I needed was to get some distance between us, so I blocked

I was in a dark, deserted parking lot when I met with the Lakota people that fateful night.

him and stepped back. With room for action I pulled my revolver from its tacky rubber pocket holster. Assaulting a presumably unarmed lawyer was worth the fight for him. Answering to a Smith & Wesson .357 magnum was not.

He retreated toward his pickup truck.

Not wanting to shoot anyone, but also needing help and not wanting to get run over by this lunatic or have him come back with a weapon, I fired a warning shot to get attention. It is illegal to discharge a gun in most places—a warning shot in public can land you in jail. But it was not illegal at that moment, on rural private property in the middle of an isolated Indian reservation. I screamed "I NEED HELP," as I fired the handgun, then jumped into my car and waited with the window down, revolver at the ready, with only four rounds left in the five round cylinder.

One of my friends at that meeting came running out. He knew my assailant. He talked to him for some time, then finally told him to leave and to never come back. Just to be sure I was safe, my friend drove his car behind me and the two of us caravanned off the reservation.

Later I learned that my attacker was a known rapist and murderer.

CHAPTER 10:

WHAT IF?

Shortly after the carnage at 101 California Street, a fellow said to me "If someone had had their conceal carry permit they could have saved a lot of people." At the time I scoffed and was terribly offended. But having been near fleeing felons, having lived in the same neighborhood where men were killed and women were raped by home invaders, and having faced down my own roving psychopath with the help of a handgun in a dark parking lot, I have changed my mind. We will never know for certain, but one armed citizen out of the hundreds working on the few floors at 101 California Street might have taken down the unskilled gunman and saved many lives.

What if a good guy had a gun?

It's a question every American needs to ask themselves; might it make a difference? If I had a handgun inside that secret file room at 101 California, and if the gunman had come in, it would have made a big difference. That I know.

Firearm bans have affected members of my family before, and the effects sometimes haunt me as much as the memories of 101 California Street. My grandfather immigrated to America in 1920, leaving most of his family in the old country. Gun control there was rigorous but selective. "Undesirable" people were disarmed, all under the banner of "safety" and "national unity." They took guns away from everyone in his neighborhood. The government said that public safety had been improved after Kristalnacht when my disarmed uncle and his remaining family were herded into trains and enslaved in concentration camps. By some miracle he survived and was brought to the United States by his brother. He remained forever clear about the inevitable disastrous result of disarming civilians.

So, what if?

CHAPTER 11:

COMING TO TERMS

It has been a long road from rallying San Franciscans and fellow lawyers to come up with more and more extreme gun control laws, to being an equally passionate advocate against such ill-conceived and unconstitutional legislation.

Time, distance and perspective have brought me clarity about my own beliefs—and a unique understanding of my own fears.

Fear motivates people. Fear is primal. Fear pushes people past rational thought to emotional reaction. That's why politicians use fear and the false promise of safety, to get votes. Trial lawyers know that they need to first convince juries on an emotional level, then let the jury justify its emotional decisions with logic retroactively constructed to justify it. Most people function that way. Fear works.

Fear of dying, of not surviving, is the greatest of all fears. And that is the blinding fear I first felt as a madman terrorized the law offices at 101 California Street in San Francisco. Knowing that I too could have been among the dead terrified me, and pushed me past any judicious analysis—on to being a gun control advocate. I wanted to feel as if I was doing something that would stop gun violence. I wanted to feel safe.

The same threat of violence followed me to Seattle, Hawaii, and South Dakota,—a person willing to do harm to me or my family. Those threats again brought out my underlying fear of becoming a victim. That fear motivated me in those places too, but differently.

Confronting these sequential threats, and examining the fear that came with them, ultimately provided a revealing perspective on violence in general, and on the soothing illusion of achieving a protective "safe" civilization in particular. After those threatening episodes, I finally came to realize that as much as I wanted to feel safe, I really wasn't completely safe. And no law would make me so.

The police—as hardworking and professional as they are—were absent at 101 California Street. They were elsewhere when my Hawaiian neighbors were robbed and raped. They were not in control of the criminal on the run in my Seattle suburb, nor the threatening nut in that South Dakota parking lot.

As the saying goes; when seconds count, police are just minutes away. Gun control laws take guns from the good guys, who obey the law. But criminals break the law by definition, and will always be able to get a gun. You can't take guns from good guys and think the bad guys won't get one. Indulging that kind of fantasy makes you vulnerable—and will get you killed. Making good people helpless cannot make bad people harmless.

These laws are all supposedly done in the name of limiting access to firearms by criminals. But prohibition doesn't work and has never worked for anything; Alcohol, drugs, guns. You cannot uninvent firearms. There are over 300 million of them in the United States. Though harder than ever to get now, guns have always been fairly easy to get if you are willing to break the law. And guns are easy to make. These days criminals can make one at home on a lathe or even on a 3D printer.

Politicians try to make people feel safe, even if they aren't truly safe. It pacifies the electorate, which might otherwise wake up, rise up, and throw them out of office. So they tell us the laws work, and to trust them.

But I have come to terms with the reality that no law will make me safe. And I won't be placated by some politician, or lawyer, no matter how well-intentioned, telling me it will.

Meanwhile every gun control law, no matter how well-intentioned, creates crippling and complicated restrictions imposed almost exclusively on good people who just want to protect themselves or make their neighborhoods a little safer. Accidental violations of complicated laws happen all too frequently, wrongly turning good guys into accidental bad guys.

The threatening experiences that I lived through forced me to come to terms with the reality that no one could be or would be responsible for my safety—except me. Evil's willingness to use violence against me would not be stopped by gun-control laws. Evil's ability to do violence to me existed largely because I had no meaningful means of protection or self-protection. These realizations haven't eliminated my fear of being attacked, but they confirmed for me that the only means of defeating the threats that prompted those fears was to take responsibility for my own protection.

So I have.

If nothing stops a bad guy from getting guns, then what can stop a bad guy intent on misusing one?

We should uniformly respect and defend the basic human right to fight for survival, and to access the most effective tools each individual chooses and needs for that task. Guns, usually without being fired, are used far more often to deter or prevent crime than they are misused to commit one. Guns have social utility. Overall, guns save lives. Many studies and my own life experience prove that.

Liberals pride themselves on protecting the constitutional rights of people to make individual lifestyle choices; as "abnormal" as those decisions may be considered by some. They condemn as bigots those who won't accept those choices. But don't those civil rights advocates step into those bigots' shoes when they condemn those who choose to own a gun to defend their family?

The legal community should be against violence. We all should be. But you can't wish violence away. It's an inescapable and sometimes unavoidable fact of life, and has been since Cain and Abel. Isn't it time to embrace the constitutional right to choose to own a gun to defend yourself or your family? Shouldn't they embrace this freedom, this choice, this essence of humanity and self preservation, as seriously as we embrace free speech, free worship and trial by jury? Shouldn't we all respect the Second Amendment as completely as we do the other nine?

Violence can descend on you without warning, like a cold fog bank on a warm San Francisco summer day. The potential for violence, and the decision of whether and how you will be ready to respond if faced with it, is a never-ending reality we all, literally, must try to live with. The sum of my fears is my realization I have to be ready to confront violence, if and when it confronts me. Now I am.

I have come to terms with preventing violence against me or my family, and I have addressed the need to be able to defend myself, including with a firearm if necessary. I will run, I will hide, or I will shoot if necessary. Not to kill, but to save my life.

I was on the front lines of the gun control movement. Now I fight for all of our Second Amendment rights. Perhaps some folks can consider my experiences, and join me on the road to enlightened empowerment.

This year I turned 50. For my birthday, I gave myself an AR-15 type rifle. Actually, I built it myself, choosing every part to make a custom rifle. Perfectly legal in South Dakota. California law, promoted by the LCAV, labels it an "assault weapon" and would brand me a felon just for having it. It is an awesome piece of equipment. I consider it a tool for developing the discipline of target shooting, hunting, and defending my family.

I have come to terms indeed.

CHAPTER 12:

"DO SOMETHING!"
(2019)

There continues to be a torrent of desperate calls to "Do Something!" after every mass shooting, each one seemingly more tragic than the last. I once joined in those calls back in 1993 and some of those calls led to the "Assault Weapons Ban of 1994." I regret doing so. I hope America is not about to make the same mistake again.

I called for "Background Checks" as that seemed reasonable and like 'common sense.' I had not yet considered the fact that so-called "Universal Background Checks" are really a backdoor way to assemble a digital database gun registry and such a gun registry database could and would easily be used for national civilian disarmament. I was not focused on the fact that civilian disarmament has historically, time after time, led to human rights violations and atrocities at the hands of armed government agents and/or soldiers.

Some political aspirants are actually calling for 'Australian-style' gun 'buybacks' which is just slang for confiscation and civilian disarmament in exchange for a token government check. Others are actually calling for repealing the Second Amendment so that civilian disarmament may proceed without those 'pesky' Constitutional issues getting in the way.

That's why it would be foolhardy to trust the government (or hackers) to not misuse and abuse a gun registry database. And why it is foolhardy to believe that "Universal Background Checks" will not promptly lead to "Australian Style Buybacks" which will result in forcible gun confiscation and civilian disarmament under threat of criminal arrest, seizure, prosecution and asset forfeiture. If you do not think this is not only possible, but the likely result, then I urge you to do some research on the Arms Trade Treaty that was signed by the Obama Administration but never ratified.

I was generally in support of the "Assault Weapons Ban" out of sheer ignorance at the time. I was never in support of taking away people's rights in the name of gun control but I didn't have a good understanding of the nature, extent and scope of those rights. I was a corporate lawyer not a civil rights lawyer. I just didn't understand at the time that banning weapons based on their look and accessories without any consideration of actual lethality was wrongheaded and ineffective.

Almost all murders are by handguns not rifles. I didn't know that an old wood stock hunting rifle is far more lethal than the mean looking black rifles that were banned. Now I know that there are upwards of 300 million firearms in private hands, a large percentage of those are black rifles and variants and there is no way to go back in time. Nor would we want to go back. These weapons are a blessing in disguise.

And if a bad situation were to happen and it does from time to time (power outage, terrorist attack, natural disaster, etc. - *i.e.*, Katrina-level or 500 year flood), most people will have a need for them to defend themselves and their families and will be happy to have them available as needed. And some people will be happy to have a few extras around to provide their neighbors with a chance of survival. The notion that it should be illegal to loan a rifle to a neighbor during times of natural disaster is contrary to the fundamental human right to live and survive.

Put another way, calls for "Do Something" led to a 10-year ban that was counterproductive to civil liberty, unjustly undermined the innate human right described above and had zero (0) impact on so-called "Gun Violence."

The same thing is going on at this very moment in 2019 and the result will be the same, or worse: ineffective laws that make people less able to defend themselves and their families from being murdered while empowering criminals and/or authoritarian government with overwhelming fire-power compared to law-abiding civilians.

Sadly, there is such a thing as evil in the World. People define evil differently; to me, it is any force that would seek to kill or seriously injure people, including me or any member of my family, because of who we are, how we look, our religion, or because we simply are in the 'wrong place' at the 'wrong time.'

Evil does not know reason. Evil can be stopped by the judicious use of lethal force. Wrongful use of lethal force has a remedy in our legal system. Intentionally depriving people of their right to stop evil coming at them does not.

Your biggest weapon is your brain. Situational awareness can save your life as it has mine. Sometimes situational awareness and your brain are not sufficient. The most effective, utilitarian and egalitarian tool to defend oneself and one's family is and has been the possession and use of modern semi-automatic firearms - handguns and long guns.

What can be done? Each individual can use their brain to attempt to avoid the evil and use their body to step around it, and run from it. Find a good hiding spot and prepare to fight for your life. Unless you are a sworn and trained officer, it's not your job to run to the gunfire; it's your job to run away from it and save yourself and your family.

I believe that if you can't run, then fight to live because your family - someone who cares about you, wants to see you again and you want to see them. If it comes to that, bludgeoning is messy business and a firearm is the most useful and effective tool to stop the fight if you are capable of handling it safely.

It is the great equalizer for the simple reason that no one wants to get shot. That is how an elderly person in a wheelchair can defend against a large assailant. That is why the vast majority of defensive gun uses only involve brandishing and not the discharge of the weapon.

Depriving people of lethal tools to stop evil coming at themselves and their families is unconscionable.

Whether done by regulations intended to squelch the right, taxation intended to make exercise of the right unaffordable, 'Red Flag' laws (which may be well intentioned but which can be misused by false accusations and lack of due process as the ACLU has recently observed), statutory technicalities, or the like, it is simply unconscionable. To do so while standing on fresh corpses is beyond unconscionable.

In times of great flux and societal crisis, deliberate speed is called for - not rushes to action for the sake of 'Doing Something.' Rushing to undermine the civil and human rights of others should be stopped.

If you want to "Do Something," get a tactical tourniquet and learn how to use it and carry it so you are able to save a life. Learn basic first aid. Carry an Individual First Aid Kit (IFAK) and know how to use it.

If you are able, acquire a firearm and learn how to use it safely and to protect your family with it. Teach your children about firearm safety and situational awareness. There are many ways to make a meaningful contribution and to "Do Something" positive.

Coming to terms with "Doing Something" positive that does not undermine the rights of others is challenging but it is the only way out of the impasse, in my opinion. The work is difficult, there are no quick fixes or 'silver bullets' but it is possible if the human right is recognized and respected.

Without respect for the human right involved, there will likely be no progress.

Illustration of the "Survivorship Bias" Phenomenon

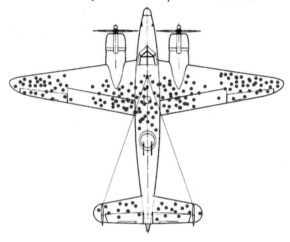

This picture shows the location of bullet holes on Allied planes that made it home after encountering Nazi fire in World War II. When shown this picture, the military initially sought to reinforce the areas marked by bullet holes because that is where they saw the most damage on returning planes. But Abraham Wald, a Hungarian-born Jewish mathematician, pointed out that the places with the dots represent the damage on the planes *that made it home*. He instructed the Allies to armor the areas where there are *no* dots because they represent the places where the planes will not survive when hit.

The military's logical error is part of a phenomenon called "survivorship bias." It is where people fail to sufficiently examine the things that did not survive and/or the reasons behind the lack of survival. This is a widespread and common phenomenon. Survivorship bias is at work when we focus on the gun(s) that were at the scene causing harm and not the gun(s) that were missing that could have been in the hands of survivors defending themselves and others against the shooter.

CHAPTER 13:

EPILOGUE
(2019)

No one believed. They listened at his heart.
Little—less—nothing!—and that ended it.
No more to build on there. And they, since they
Were not the one dead, turned to their affairs.
—Robert Frost - "Out, Out-" (1916)

"And they, since they were not the one dead, turned to their affairs." No truer words have ever been uttered.

I am particularly grateful to be alive to write this and so is my family. Others were not so lucky. I don't know why some make it and some don't. That is above my pay grade. I know that I have wept for those who didn't survive and, occasionally, I still shed a tear for one of my lost friends or colleagues.

This is my personal opinion: Each human has the innate right to prevent their own murder and to prevent serious injury being done to them and their families. Do you agree?

If so, perhaps you will agree that such right may not be infringed to the same extent that other innate human rights may not be infringed.

Further, I believe that the human right to prevent one's own murder, rape or other injury includes the right of armed self defense and defense of one's families and loved ones.

Finally, I believe that such human right also includes a right to possess and use commonly available lethal tools if the person exercising such right is capable of telling right from wrong and of using such tools safely.

These lethal tools include Modern Sporting Rifles also known as AR and AK type rifles, semi-automatic handguns, magazines of all sizes, accessories of all kinds and all calibers (as it is not for anyone to judge how many rounds are needed by a particular individual to prevent others from doing them serious harm). This includes the right to carry, concealed or openly, weapons for self defense and defense of others in public, and that right should be respected at least, if not more, than a drivers' license is respected from state-to-state.

Sadly, not every human can tell right from wrong. Some are insane, others are mentally disabled. Not every human can safely use lethal tools. Some are not well-suited to making life and death decisions; some are not physically capable (e.g., a blind person not being able to see the target). It is impossible to predict every situation.

But if laws and law enforcement are to parse who can tell right from wrong and who can be expected to safely possess and use lethal tools, then government abuse seems inevitable. Especially when government officials are motivated to take matters into their own hands in order to "Do Something."

Due process is a concept that is given such short shrift in our modern federal court system. As a result, there is little faith that such laws will be fairly applied to gun owners. We are at a societal impasse.

It is time for us to come to terms first with common agreements that:

- Each human has the innate right to prevent their own murder and to prevent serious injury being done to them and their families;
- Using commonly available lethal tools if the person exercising such right is capable of telling right from wrong and of using such tools safely; which tools include semi-automatic handguns and rifles (including AR and AK type rifles), magazines of all sizes, accessories of all kinds and all calibers; and which
- Includes the right to carry, concealed or openly, weapons for self defense and defense of others in public.

Do you agree?

ABOUT THE AUTHOR

 **David Frankel** has been a lawyer since 1990 specializing in business law, intellectual property (copyrights, trademarks, trade secrets), startups, small business financing, private offerings, contracts, federal 'Indian' law, civil and human rights projects, federal administrative, nonprofits, and government licensing proceedings. Mr. Frankel currently serves as a volunteer on several member committees of the California Rifle and Pistol Association.

In 1989-1990, Mr. Frankel was recruited out of NYU Law School to join the Corporate Law department of what was then a large San Francisco law firm called Pettit & Martin. Working long hours, he learned the ropes and intricacies of corporations, partnerships, mergers & acquisitions, hostile takeovers, private and public offerings, fiduciary and banking law, federal administrative matters, and copyrights, trademarks, and licensing law. That changed with the experience of surviving the law firm shootings at 101 California Street on July 1, 1993.

After recovering from the shock and trauma of losing friends and colleagues to the mass shooter's violence, Mr. Frankel changed course and switched to a boutique San Francisco law firm where he practiced business and corporate law. At the end of the associate track, Mr. Frankel was offered a partnership position but turned it down in order to start his own independent law practice and focus more time on human rights, civil rights and environmental concerns than would be appropriate in a law firm partnership setting.

Since 1998, Mr. Frankel has maintained an independent law firm including a large percentage of pro bono work for the benefit of civil rights organizations, tribal members, community and/or environmental organizations for the benefit of people's liberty, freedom, civil rights, constitutionally protected rights, and human rights.

After the 2008 *Heller* decision by the US Supreme Court, Mr. Frankel focused time and energy in a concerted effort to better understand the nature and extent of the Right to Keep and Bear Arms, as protected by the Second Amendment, as a fundamental individual human right. Mr. Frankel is one of a handful of pro-gun rights survivors of mass shootings, a Lifetime Member of the NRA, a member of the California Rifle and Pistol Association, and several other organizations that act in support of the innate human Right to Keep and Bear Arms.

Feel free to contact David Frankel by email at info@davidfrankel.org.

Appendix:

Heller v. District Of Columbia
MAJORITY OPINION

128 S.Ct. 2783
Supreme Court of the United States
DISTRICT OF COLUMBIA et al., Petitioners,

v.

Dick Anthony HELLER.
No. 07–290.
Argued March 18, 2008. Decided June 26, 2008.

SYNOPSIS

Background: Special police officer and others brought action seeking, on Second Amendment grounds, to enjoin District of Columbia from enforcing gun-control statutes. The United States District Court for the District of Columbia, Sullivan, J., 311 F.Supp.2d 103, granted District of Columbia's motion to dismiss, and appeal was taken. The District of Columbia Court of Appeals, Silberman, Senior Circuit Judge, 478 F.3d 370, reversed. Certiorari was granted.

Opinion

Justice SCALIA delivered the opinion of the Court.

We consider whether a District of Columbia prohibition on the possession of usable handguns in the home violates the Second Amendment to the Constitution.

I

The District of Columbia generally prohibits the possession of handguns. It is a crime to carry an unregistered firearm, and the registration of handguns is prohibited. See D.C. Code §§ 7–2501.01(12), 7–2502.01(a), 7–2502.02(a)(4) (2001). Wholly apart from that prohibition, no person may carry a handgun without a license, but the chief of police may issue licenses for 1–year periods. See §§ 22–4504(a), 22–4506. District of Columbia law also requires residents to keep their lawfully owned firearms, such as registered long guns, "unloaded and dissembled or bound by a trigger lock or similar device" unless they are located in a place of business or are being used for lawful recreational activities. See § 7–2507.02.[1]

Respondent Dick Heller is a D.C. special police officer authorized to carry a handgun while on duty at the Thurgood Marshall Judiciary Building. He applied for a registration certificate for a handgun that he wished to keep at home, but the District refused. He thereafter filed a lawsuit in the Federal District Court for the District of Columbia seeking, on Second Amendment grounds, to enjoin the city from enforcing the bar on the registration of handguns, the licensing requirement insofar as

---

[1] There are minor exceptions to all of these prohibitions, none of which is relevant here.

it prohibits the carrying of a firearm in the home without a license, and the trigger-lock requirement insofar as it prohibits the use of "functional firearms within the home." App. 59a. The District Court dismissed respondent's complaint, see *Parker v. District of Columbia*, 311 F.Supp.2d 103, 109 (2004). The Court of Appeals for the District of Columbia Circuit, construing his complaint as seeking the right to render a firearm operable and carry it about his home in that condition only when necessary for self-defense,[2] reversed, see *Parker v. District of Columbia*, 478 F.3d 370, 401 (2007). It held that the Second Amendment protects an individual right to possess firearms and that the city's total ban on handguns, as well as its requirement that firearms in the home be kept nonfunctional even when necessary for self-defense, violated that right. See *id.*, at 395, 399–401. The Court of Appeals directed the District Court to enter summary judgment for respondent.

We granted certiorari. 552 U.S. 1035, 128 S.Ct. 645, 169 L.Ed.2d 417 (2007).

II

We turn first to the meaning of the Second Amendment

A

The Second Amendment provides: "A well regulated Militia, being necessary to the security of a free State, the right of the people to keep and bear Arms, shall not be infringed." In interpreting this text, we are guided

---

[2] That construction has not been challenged here.

Petitioners and today's dissenting Justices believe that it protects only the right to possess and carry a firearm in connection with militia service.

---

by the principle that "[t]he Constitution was written to be understood by the voters; its words and phrases were used in their normal and ordinary as distinguished from technical meaning." *United States v. Sprague,* 282 U.S. 716, 731, 51 S.Ct. 220, 75 L.Ed. 640 (1931); see also *Gibbons v. Ogden,* 9 Wheat. 1, 188, 6 L.Ed. 23 (1824). Normal meaning may of course include an idiomatic meaning, but it excludes secret or technical meanings that would not have been known to ordinary citizens in the founding generation.

The two sides in this case have set out very different interpretations of the Amendment. Petitioners and today's dissenting Justices believe that it protects only the right to possess and carry a firearm in connection with militia service. See Brief for Petitioners 11–12; post, at 2822 (STEVENS, J., dissenting). Respondent argues that it protects an individual right to possess a firearm unconnected with service in a militia, and to use that arm for traditionally lawful purposes, such as self-defense within the home. See Brief for Respondent 2–4.

The Second Amendment is naturally divided into two parts: its prefatory clause and its operative clause. The former does not limit the latter grammatically, but rather announces a purpose. The Amendment could be rephrased, "Because a well regulated Militia is necessary to the security of a free State, the right of the people to keep and bear Arms shall not be infringed." See J.

> *Respondent argues that it protects an individual right to possess a firearm unconnected with service in a militia, and to use that arm for traditionally lawful purposes, such as self-defense within the home.*

Tiffany, A Treatise on Government and Constitutional Law § 585, p. 394 (1867); Brief for Professors of Linguistics and English as *Amici Curiae* 3 (hereinafter Linguists' Brief). Although this structure of the Second Amendment is unique in our Constitution, other legal documents of the founding era, particularly individual-rights provisions of state constitutions, commonly included a prefatory statement of purpose. See generally Volokh, The Commonplace Second Amendment, 73 N.Y.U.L.Rev. 793, 814–821 (1998).

Logic demands that there be a link between the stated purpose and the command. The Second Amendment would be nonsensical if it read, "A well regulated Militia, being necessary to the security of a free State, the right of the people to petition for redress of grievances shall not be infringed." That requirement of logical connection may cause a prefatory clause to resolve an ambiguity in the operative clause. ("The separation of church and state being an important objective, the teachings of canons shall have no place in our jurisprudence." The preface makes clear that the operative clause refers not to canons of interpretation but to clergymen.) But apart from that clarifying function, a prefatory clause does not limit or expand the scope of the operative clause. See F. Dwarris, A General Treatise on Statutes 268–269 (P. Potter ed. 1871); T. Sedgwick, The Interpretation and Construction of

Statutory and Constitutional Law 42–45 (2d ed. 1874).[3]
"'It is nothing unusual in acts ... for the enacting part
to go beyond the preamble; the remedy often extends
beyond the particular act or mischief which first suggested the necessity of the law.'" J. Bishop, Commentaries
on Written Laws and Their Interpretation § 51, p. 49
(1882) (quoting *Rex v. Marks*, 3 East 157, 165, 102 Eng.
Rep. 557, 560 (K.B.1802)). Therefore, while we will begin our textual analysis with the operative clause, we will
return to the prefatory clause to ensure that our reading
of the operative clause is consistent with the announced
purpose.[4]

---

[3] As Sutherland explains, the key 18th-century English case on the effect of preambles, *Copeman v. Gallant*, 1 P. Wms. 314, 24 Eng. Rep.
404 (1716), stated that "the preamble could not be used to restrict the
effect of the words used in the purview." 2A N. Singer, Sutherland on
Statutory Construction § 47.04, pp. 145–146 (rev. 5th ed.1992). This
rule was modified in England in an 1826 case to give more importance
to the preamble, but in America "the settled principle of law is that the
preamble cannot control the enacting part of the statute in cases where
the enacting part is expressed in clear, unambiguous terms." *Id.*, at 146.

Justice STEVENS says that we violate the general rule that every
clause in a statute must have effect. *Post*, at 2826. But where the text
of a clause itself indicates that it does not have operative effect, such as
"whereas" clauses in federal legislation or the Constitution's preamble,
a court has no license to make it do what it was not designed to do. Or
to put the point differently, operative provisions should be given effect
as operative provisions, and prologues as prologues.

[4] Justice STEVENS criticizes us for discussing the prologue last. *Ibid.*
But if a prologue can be used only to clarify an ambiguous operative
provision, surely the first step must be to determine whether the operative provision is ambiguous. It might be argued, we suppose, that the
prologue itself should be one of the factors that go into the determination of whether the operative provision is ambiguous—but that would
cause the prologue to be used to produce ambiguity rather than just to
resolve it. In any event, even if we considered the prologue *along with*
the operative provision we would reach the same result we do today,
since (as we explain) our interpretation of "the right of the people to
keep and bear arms" furthers the purpose of an effective militia no

1. Operative Clause.

a. "Right of the People." The first salient feature of the operative clause is that it codifies a "right of the people." The unamended Constitution and the Bill of Rights use the phrase "right of the people" two other times, in the First Amendment's Assembly–and–Petition Clause and in the Fourth Amendment's Search–and–Seizure Clause. The Ninth Amendment uses very similar terminology ("The enumeration in the Constitution, of certain rights, shall not be construed to deny or disparage others retained by the people"). All three of these instances unambiguously refer to individual rights, not "collective" rights, or rights that may be exercised only through participation in some corporate body.[5]

Three provisions of the Constitution refer to "the people" in a context other than "rights"—the famous preamble ("We the people"), § 2 of Article I (providing that "the people" will choose members of the House), and the Tenth Amendment (providing that those powers not given the Federal Government remain with "the States" or "the people"). Those provisions arguably refer to "the people" acting collectively— but they deal with the exercise or reservation of powers, not rights. Nowhere

---

less than (indeed, more than) the dissent's interpretation. See *infra*, at 2801–2802.

[5] Justice STEVENS is of course correct, *post,* at 2827, that the right to assemble cannot be exercised alone, but it is still an individual right, and not one conditioned upon membership in some defined "assembly," as he contends the right to bear arms is conditioned upon membership in a defined militia. And Justice STEVENS is dead wrong to think that the right to petition is "primarily collective in nature." *Ibid.* See *McDonald v. Smith*, 472 U.S. 479, 482–484, 105 S.Ct. 2787, 86 L.Ed.2d 384 (1985) (describing historical origins of right to petition).

else in the Constitution does a "right" attributed to "the people" refer to anything other than an individual right.[6]

What is more, in all six other provisions of the Constitution that mention "the people," the term unambiguously refers to all members of the political community, not an unspecified subset. As we said in *United States v. Verdugo–Urquidez*, 494 U.S. 259, 265, 110 S.Ct. 1056, 108 L.Ed.2d 222 (1990):

> "'[T]he people' seems to have been a term of art employed in select parts of the Constitution ... [Its uses] sugges[t] that 'the people' protected by the Fourth Amendment, and by the First and Second Amendments, and to whom rights and powers are reserved in the Ninth and Tenth Amendments, refers to a class of persons who are part of a national community or who have otherwise developed sufficient connection with this country to be considered part of that community."

---

[6] If we look to other founding-era documents, we find that some state constitutions used the term "the people" to refer to the people collectively, in contrast to "citizen," which was used to invoke individual rights. See Heyman, Natural Rights and the Second Amendment, in The Second Amendment in Law and History 179, 193–195 (C. Bogus ed.2000) (hereinafter Bogus). But that usage was not remotely uniform. See, *e.g.*, N.C. Declaration of Rights § XIV (1776), in 5 The Federal and State Constitutions, Colonial Charters, and Other Organic Laws 2787, 2788 (F. Thorpe ed.1909) (hereinafter Thorpe) (jury trial); Md. Declaration of Rights § XVIII (1776), in 3 *id.*, at 1686, 1688 (vicinage requirement); Vt. Declaration of Rights, ch. 1, § XI (1777), in 6 *id.*, at 3737, 3741 (searches and seizures); Pa. Declaration of Rights § XII (1776), in 5 *id.*, at 3082, 3083 (free speech). And, most importantly, it was clearly not the terminology used in the Federal Constitution, given the First, Fourth, and Ninth Amendments.

This contrasts markedly with the phrase "the militia" in the prefatory clause. As we will describe below, the "militia" in colonial America consisted of a subset of "the people"—those who were male, able bodied, and within a certain age range. Reading the Second Amendment as protecting only the right to "keep and bear Arms" in an organized militia therefore fits poorly with the operative clause's description of the holder of that right as "the people."

We start therefore with a strong presumption that the Second Amendment right is exercised individually and belongs to all Americans.

b. "Keep and Bear Arms." We move now from the holder of the right—"the people"—to the substance of the right: "to keep and bear Arms."

Before addressing the verbs "keep" and "bear," we interpret their object: "Arms." The 18th-century meaning is no different from the meaning today. The 1773 edition of Samuel Johnson's dictionary defined "arms" as "[w]eapons of offence, or armour of defence." 1 Dictionary of the English Language 106 (4th ed.) (reprinted 1978) (hereinafter Johnson). Timothy Cunningham's important 1771 legal dictionary defined "arms" as "any thing that a man wears for his defence, or takes into his hands, or useth in wrath to cast at or strike another." 1 A New and Complete Law Dictionary; see also N. Webster, American Dictionary of the English Language (1828) (reprinted 1989) (hereinafter Webster) (similar).

The term was applied, then as now, to weapons that were not specifically designed for military use and were not employed in a military capacity. For instance, Cunningham's legal dictionary gave as an example of usage: "Servants and labourers shall use bows and arrows on *Sundays*, & c. and not bear other arms." See also, e.g., An Act for the trial of Negroes, 1797 Del. Laws ch. XLIII, § 6, in 1 First Laws of the State of Delaware 102, 104 (J. Cushing ed.1981 (pt. 1)); see generally *State v. Duke*, 42 Tex. 455, 458 (1874) (citing decisions of state courts construing "arms"). Although one founding-era thesaurus limited "arms" (as opposed to "weapons") to "instruments of offence generally made use of in war," even that source stated that all firearms constituted "arms." 1 J. Trusler, The Distinction Between Words Esteemed Synonymous in the English Language 37 (3d ed. 1794) (emphasis added).

Some have made the argument, bordering on the frivolous, that only those arms in existence in the 18th century are protected by the Second Amendment. We do not interpret constitutional rights that way. Just as the First Amendment protects modern forms of communications, *e.g., Reno v. American Civil Liberties Union*, 521 U.S. 844, 849, 117 S.Ct. 2329, 138 L.Ed.2d 874 (1997), and the Fourth Amendment applies to modern forms of search, e.g., *Kyllo v. United States*, 533 U.S. 27, 35–36, 121 S.Ct. 2038, 150 L.Ed.2d 94 (2001), the Second Amendment extends, prima facie, to all instruments that constitute bearable arms, even those that were not in existence at the time of the founding.

We turn to the phrases "keep arms" and "bear arms." Johnson defined "keep" as, most relevantly, "[t]o retain; not to lose," and "[t]o have in custody." Johnson 1095. Webster defined it as "[t]o hold; to retain in one's power or possession." No party has apprised us of an idiomatic meaning of "keep Arms." Thus, the most natural reading of "keep Arms" in the Second Amendment is to "have weapons."

The phrase "keep arms" was not prevalent in the written documents of the founding period that we have found, but there are a few examples, all of which favor viewing the right to "keep Arms" as an individual right unconnected with militia service. William Blackstone, for example, wrote that Catholics convicted of not attending service in the Church of England suffered certain penalties, one of which was that they were not permitted to "keep arms in their houses." 4 Commentaries on the Laws of England 55 (1769) (hereinafter Blackstone); see also 1 W. & M., ch. 15, § 4, in 3 Eng. Stat. at Large 422 (1689) ("[N]o Papist ... shall or may have or keep in his House ... any Arms ..."); 1 W. Hawkins, Treatise on the Pleas of the Crown 26 (1771) (similar). Petitioners point to militia laws of the founding period that required militia members to "keep" arms in connection with militia service, and they conclude from this that the phrase "keep Arms" has a militia-related connotation. See Brief for Petitioners 16–17 (citing laws of Delaware, New Jersey, and Virginia). This is rather like saying that, since there are many statutes that authorize aggrieved employees to "file complaints" with federal agencies, the phrase "file complaints" has an employment-related connotation. "Keep arms" was simply a common way of referring to possessing arms, for militiamen *and everyone else*.[7]

---

[7] See, e.g., 3 A Compleat Collection of State–Tryals 185 (1719) ("Hath not every Subject power to keep Arms, as well as Servants in his House for defence of his Person?"); T. Wood, A New Institute of the

At the time of the founding, as now, to "bear" meant to "carry." See Johnson 161; Webster; T. Sheridan, A Complete Dictionary of the English Language (1796); 2 Oxford English Dictionary 20 (2d ed.1989) (hereinafter Oxford). When used with "arms," however, the term has a meaning that refers to carrying for a particular purpose—confrontation. In *Muscarello v. United States*, 524

Imperial or Civil Law 282 (1730) ("Those are guilty of *publick* Force, who keep Arms in their Houses, and make use of them otherwise than upon Journeys or Hunting, or for Sale ..."); A Collection of All the Acts of Assembly, Now in Force, in the Colony of Virginia 596 (1733) ("Free Negros, Mulattos, or Indians, and Owners of Slaves, seated at Frontier Plantations, may obtain Licence from a Justice of Peace, for keeping Arms, &c."); J. Ayliffe, A New Pandect of *Roman* Civil Law 195 (1734) ("Yet a Person might keep Arms in his House, or on his Estate, on the Account of Hunting, Navigation, Travelling, and on the Score of Selling them in the way of Trade or Commerce, or such Arms as accrued to him by way of Inheritance"); J. Trusler, A Concise View of the Common Law and Statute Law of England 270 (1781) ("[I]f [papists] keep arms in their houses, such arms may be seized by a justice of the peace"); Some Considerations on the Game Laws 54 (1796) ("Who has been deprived by [the law] of keeping arms for his own defence? What law forbids the veriest pauper, if he can raise a sum sufficient for the purchase of it, from mounting his Gun on his Chimney Piece ... ?"); 3 B. Wilson, The Works of the Honourable James Wilson 84 (1804) (with reference to state constitutional right: "This is one of our many renewals of the Saxon regulations. 'They were bound,' says Mr. Selden, 'to keep arms for the preservation of the kingdom, and of their own persons' "); W. Duer, Outlines of the Constitutional Jurisprudence of the United States 31–32 (1833) (with reference to colonists' English rights: "The right of every individual to keep arms for his defence, suitable to his condition and degree; which was the public allowance, under due restrictions of the natural right of resistance and self-preservation"); 3 R. Burn, Justice of Peace and Parish Officer 88 (29th ed. 1845) ("It is, however, laid down by Serjeant *Hawkins*,... that if a lessee, after the end of the term, keep arms in his house to oppose the entry of the lessor, ..."); *State v. Dempsey*, 31 N.C. 384, 385 (1849) (citing 1840 state law making it a misdemeanor for a member of certain racial groups "to carry about his person or keep in his house any shot gun or other arms").

U.S. 125, 118 S.Ct. 1911, 141 L.Ed.2d 111 (1998), in the course of analyzing the meaning of "carries a firearm" in a federal criminal statute, Justice GINSBURG wrote that "[s]urely a most familiar meaning is, as the Constitution's Second Amendment... indicate[s]: 'wear, bear, or carry... upon the person or in the clothing or in a pocket, for the purpose... of being armed and ready for offensive or defensive action in a case of conflict with another person.'" *Id.*, at 143, 118 S.Ct. 1911 (dissenting opinion) (quoting Black's Law Dictionary 214 (6th ed.1990)). We think that Justice GINSBURG accurately captured the natural meaning of "bear arms." Although the phrase implies that the carrying of the weapon is for the purpose of "offensive or defensive action," it in no way connotes participation in a structured military organization.

From our review of founding-era sources, we conclude that this natural meaning was also the meaning that "bear arms" had in the 18th century. In numerous instances, "bear arms" was unambiguously used to refer to the carrying of weapons outside of an organized militia. The most prominent examples are those most relevant to the Second Amendment: nine state constitutional provisions written in the 18th century or the first two decades of the 19th, which enshrined a right of citizens to "bear arms in defense of themselves and the state" or "bear arms in defense of himself and the

---

In numerous instances, "bear arms" was unambiguously used to refer to the carrying of weapons outside of an organized militia.

---

state."[8] It is clear from those formulations that "bear arms" did not refer only to carrying a weapon in an organized military unit. Justice James Wilson interpreted the Pennsylvania Constitution's arms-bearing right, for example, as a recognition of the natural right of defense "of one's person or house"—what he called the law of "self preservation." 2 Collected Works of James Wilson 1142, and n. x (K. Hall & M. Hall eds.2007) (citing Pa. Const., Art. IX, § 21 (1790)); see also T. Walker, Introduction to American Law 198 (1837) ("Thus the right of self-defence [is] guaranteed by the [Ohio] constitution"); see also *id.*, at 157 (equating Second Amendment with that provision of the Ohio Constitution). That was also the interpretation of those state constitutional provisions adopted by pre-Civil War state courts.[9] These provisions

---

[8] See Pa. Declaration of Rights § XIII, in 5 Thorpe 3083 ("That the people have a right to bear arms for the defence of themselves and the state... "); Vt. Declaration of Rights, ch. 1, § XV, in 6 *id.*, at 3741 ("That the people have a right to bear arms for the defence of themselves and the State ..."); Ky. Const., Art. XII, § 23 (1792), in 3 *id.*, at 1264, 1275 ("That the right of the citizens to bear arms in defence of themselves and the State shall not be questioned"); Ohio Const., Art. VIII, § 20 (1802), in 5 *id.*, at 2901, 2911 ("That the people have a right to bear arms for the defence of themselves and the State... "); Ind. Const., Art. First, § 20 (1816), in 2 *id.*, at 1057, 1059 ("That the people have a right to bear arms for the defense of themselves and the State... "); Miss. Const., Art. I, § 23 (1817), in 4 *id.*, at 2032, 2034 ("Every citizen has a right to bear arms, in defense of himself and the State"); Conn. Const., Art. First, § 17 (1818), in *id.*, at 536, 538 ("Every citizen has a right to bear arms in defense of himself and the state"); Ala. Const., Art. I, § 23 (1819), in *id.*, at 96, 98 ("Every citizen has a right to bear arms in defence of himself and the State"); Mo. Const., Art. XIII, § 3 (1820), in 4 *id.*, at 2150, 2163 ("[T]hat their right to bear arms in defence of themselves and of the State cannot be questioned"). See generally Volokh, State Constitutional Rights to Keep and Bear Arms, 11 Tex. Rev. L. & Politics 191 (2006).

[9] See *Bliss v. Commonwealth*, 12 Ky. 90, 2 Litt. 90, 91–92 (1822); *State v. Reid*, 1 Ala. 612, 616–617 (1840); *State v. Schoultz*, 25 Mo. 128,

demonstrate—again, in the most analogous linguistic context—that "bear arms" was not limited to the carrying of arms in a militia.

The phrase "bear Arms" also had at the time of the founding an idiomatic meaning that was significantly different from its natural meaning: "to serve as a soldier, do military service, fight" or "to wage war." See Linguists' Brief 18; *post*, at 2827–2828 (STEVENS, J., dissenting). But it *unequivocally* bore that idiomatic meaning only when followed by the preposition "against," which was in turn followed by the target of the hostilities. See 2 Oxford 21. (That is how, for example, our Declaration of Independence ¶ 28 used the phrase: "He has constrained our fellow Citizens taken Captive on the high Seas to bear Arms against their Country ....") Every example given by petitioners' *amici* for the idiomatic meaning of "bear arms" from the founding period either includes the preposition "against" or is not clearly idiomatic. See Linguists' Brief 18–23. Without the preposition, "bear arms" normally meant (as it continues to mean today) what Justice GINSBURG's opinion in *Muscarello* said.

In any event, the meaning of "bear arms" that petitioners and Justice STEVENS propose is *not even* the (sometimes) idiomatic meaning. Rather, they manufacture a hybrid definition, whereby "bear arms" connotes the actual carrying of arms (and therefore is not really an idiom) but only in the service of an organized militia.

---

155 (1857); see also *Simpson v. State*, 13 Tenn. 356, 5 Yer. 356, 360 (1833) (interpreting similar provision with " 'common defence' " purpose); *State v. Huntly*, 25 N.C. 418, 422–423 (1843) (same); cf. *Nunn v. State*, 1 Ga. 243, 250–251 (1846) (construing Second Amendment); *State v. Chandler*, 5 La. Ann. 489, 489–490 (1850) (same).

No dictionary has ever adopted that definition, and we have been apprised of no source that indicates that it carried that meaning at the time of the founding. But it is easy to see why petitioners and the dissent are driven to the hybrid definition. Giving "bear Arms" its idiomatic meaning would cause the protected right to consist of the right to be a soldier or to wage war—an absurdity that no commentator has ever endorsed. See L. Levy, Origins of the Bill of Rights 135 (1999). Worse still, the phrase "keep and bear Arms" would be incoherent. The word "Arms" would have two different meanings at once: "weapons" (as the object of "keep") and (as the object of "bear") one-half of an idiom. It would be rather like saying "He filled and kicked the bucket" to mean "He filled the bucket and died." Grotesque.

Petitioners justify their limitation of "bear arms" to the military context by pointing out the unremarkable fact that it was often used in that context—the same mistake they made with respect to "keep arms." It is especially unremarkable that the phrase was often used in a military context in the federal legal sources (such as records of congressional debate) that have been the focus of petitioners' inquiry. Those sources would have had little occasion to use it *except* in discussions about the standing army and the militia. And the phrases used primarily in those military discussions include not only "bear arms" but also "carry arms," "possess arms," and "have arms"—though no one thinks that those *other* phrases also had special military meanings. See Barnett, Was the Right to Keep and Bear Arms Conditioned on Service in an Organized Militia? 83 Texas L.Rev. 237, 261 (2004). The common references to those "fit to bear arms" in congressional discussions about the militia are matched by use of the same phrase in the few nonmilitary federal contexts where the concept would be relevant. See, *e.g.*, 30 Journals of Continental Congress 349–351 (J. Fitzpatrick ed.1934). Other legal sources frequently used "bear arms" in nonmilitary contexts.[10] Cunningham's legal dictionary, cited above, gave as an example of its usage a sentence unrelated to military affairs ("Servants and labourers shall use bows and arrows on *Sundays*, & c. and not bear other arms"). And if one looks beyond legal sources, "bear arms" was frequently used in nonmilitary contexts. See Cramer & Olson, What Did "Bear Arms"

---

[10] See J. Brydall, Privilegia Magnatud apud Anglos 14 (1704) (Privilege XXXIII) ("In the 21st Year of King Edward the Third, a Proclamation Issued, that no Person should bear any Arms within London, and the Suburbs"); J. Bond, A Compleat Guide to Justices of the Peace 43 (3d ed. 1707) ("Sheriffs, and all other Officers in executing their Offices, and all other persons pursuing Hu[e] and Cry may lawfully bear Arms"); 1 An Abridgment of the Public Statutes in Force and Use Relative to Scotland (1755) (entry for "Arms": "And if any person above described shall have in his custody, use, or bear arms, being thereof convicted before one justice of peace, or other judge competent, summarily, he shall for the first offense forfeit all such arms" (citing 1 Geo., ch. 54, § 1, in 5 Eng. Stat. at Large 90 (1668))); Statute Law of Scotland Abridged 132–133 (2d ed. 1769) ("Acts for disarming the highlands" but "exempting those who have particular licenses to bear arms"); E. de Vattel, The Law of Nations, or, Principles of the Law of Nature 144 (1792) ("Since custom has allowed persons of rank and gentlemen of the army to bear arms in time of peace, strict care should be taken that none but these should be allowed to wear swords"); E. Roche, Proceedings of a Court–Martial, Held at the Council–Chamber, in the City of Cork 3 (1798) (charge VI: "With having held traitorous conferences, and with having conspired, with the like intent, for the purpose of attacking and despoiling of the arms of several of the King's subjects, qualified by law to bear arms"); C. Humphreys, A Compendium of the Common Law in Force in Kentucky 482 (1822) ("[I]n this country the constitution guarranties to all persons the right to bear arms; then it can only be a crime to exercise this right in such a manner, as to terrify people unnecessarily").

Mean in the Second Amendment? 6 Georgetown J.L. & Pub. Pol'y 511 (2008) (identifying numerous nonmilitary uses of "bear arms" from the founding period).

Justice STEVENS points to a study by *amici* supposedly showing that the phrase "bear arms" was most frequently used in the military context. See *post*, at 2828–2829, n. 9; Linguists' Brief 24. Of course, as we have said, the fact that the phrase was commonly used in a particular context does not show that it is limited to that context, and, in any event, we have given many sources where the phrase was used in nonmilitary contexts. Moreover, the study's collection appears to include (who knows how many times) the idiomatic phrase "bear arms against," which is irrelevant. The *amici* also dismiss examples such as " 'bear arms... for the purpose of killing game'" because those uses are "expressly qualified." Linguists' Brief 24. (Justice STEVENS uses the same excuse for dismissing the state constitutional provisions analogous to the Second Amendment that identify private-use purposes for which the individual right can be asserted. See *post*, at 2828.) That analysis is faulty. A purposive qualifying phrase that contradicts the word or phrase it modifies is unknown this side of the looking glass (except, apparently, in some courses on linguistics). If "bear arms" means, as we think, simply the carrying of arms, a modifier can limit the purpose of the carriage ("for the purpose of self-defense" or "to make war against the King"). But if "bear arms" means, as the petitioners and the dissent think, the carrying of arms only for military purposes, one simply cannot add "for the purpose of killing game." The right "to carry arms in the militia for the purpose of killing game" is worthy of the Mad Hat-

ter. Thus, these purposive qualifying phrases positively establish that "to bear arms" is not limited to military use.[11]

Justice STEVENS places great weight on James Madison's inclusion of a conscientious-objector clause in his original draft of the Second Amendment: "but no person religiously scrupulous of bearing arms, shall be compelled to render military service in person." Creating the Bill of Rights 12 (H. Veit, K. Bowling, & C. Bickford eds.1991) (hereinafter Veit). He argues that this clause establishes that the drafters of the Second Amendment intended "bear Arms" to refer only to military service. *See post*, at 2836. It is always perilous to derive the meaning of an adopted provision from another provision deleted in the drafting process.[12] In any case, what Justice STEVENS would conclude from the deleted provision does not follow. It was not meant to exempt from military service those who objected to

---

[11] Justice STEVENS contends, *post*, at 2830, that since we assert that adding "against" to "bear arms" gives it a military meaning we must concede that adding a purposive qualifying phrase to "bear arms" can alter its meaning. But the difference is that we do not maintain that "against" *alters* the meaning of "bear arms" but merely that it *clarifies* which of various meanings (one of which is military) is intended. Justice STEVENS, however, argues that "[t]he term 'bear arms' is a familiar idiom; when used unadorned by any additional words, its meaning is 'to serve as a soldier, do military service, fight.'" *Post*, at 2828. He therefore must establish that adding a contradictory purposive phrase can alter a word's meaning.

[12] Justice STEVENS finds support for his legislative history inference from the recorded views of one Antifederalist member of the House. *Post*, at 2836, n. 25. "The claim that the best or most representative reading of the [language of the] amendments would conform to the understanding and concerns of [the Antifederalists] is... highly problematic." Rakove, The Second Amendment: The Highest Stage of Originalism, in Bogus 74, 81.

going to war but had no scruples about personal gun-
fights. Quakers opposed the use of arms not just for militia service, but for any violent purpose whatsoever—
so much so that Quaker frontiersmen were forbidden
to use arms to defend their families, even though "[i]
n such circumstances the temptation to seize a hunting
rifle or knife in self-defense ... must sometimes have been
almost overwhelming." P. Brock, Pacifism in the United
States 359 (1968); see M. Hirst, The Quakers in Peace
and War 336–339 (1923); 3 T. Clarkson, Portraiture of
Quakerism 103–104 (3d ed. 1807). The Pennsylvania
Militia Act of 1757 exempted from service those "*scru-
pling the use of arms*"—a phrase that no one contends
had an idiomatic meaning. See 5 Stat. at Large of Pa.
613 (J. Mitchell & H. Flanders comm'rs 1898) (emphasis in original). Thus, the most natural interpretation of
Madison's deleted text is that those opposed to carrying
weapons for potential violent confrontation would not
be "compelled to render military service," in which such
carrying would be required.[13]

Finally, Justice STEVENS suggests that "keep and
bear Arms" was some sort of term of art, presumably

---

[13] The same applies to the conscientious-objector amendments proposed by Virginia and North Carolina, which said: "That any person
religiously scrupulous of bearing arms ought to be exempted upon pay-
ment of an equivalent to employ another to bear arms in his stead."
See Veit 19; 4 J. Eliot, The Debates in the Several State Constitutions
on the Adoption of the Federal Constitution 243, 244 (2d ed. 1836)
(reprinted 1941). Certainly their second use of the phrase ("bear arms
in his stead") refers, by reason of context, to compulsory bearing of
arms for military duty. But their first use of the phrase ("any person religiously scrupulous of bearing arms") assuredly did not refer to people
whose God allowed them to bear arms for defense of themselves but
not for defense of their country.

akin to "hue and cry" or "cease and desist." (This suggestion usefully evades the problem that there is no evidence whatsoever to support a military reading of "keep arms.") Justice STEVENS believes that the unitary meaning of "keep and bear Arms" is established by the Second Amendment's calling it a "right" (singular) rather than "rights" (plural). See *post*, at 2830–2831. There is nothing to this. State constitutions of the founding period routinely grouped multiple (related) guarantees under a singular "right," and the First Amendment protects the "right [singular] of the people peaceably to assemble, and to petition the Government for a redress of grievances." See, *e.g.*, Pa. Declaration of Rights §§ IX, XII, XVI, in 5 Thorpe 3083–3084; Ohio Const., Art. VIII, §§ 11, 19 (1802), in *id.*, at 2910–2911.[14] And even if "keep and bear Arms" were a unitary phrase, we find no evidence that it bore a military meaning. Although the phrase was not at all common (which would be unusual for a term of art), we have found instances of its use with a clearly nonmilitary connotation. In a 1780 debate in the House of Lords, for example, Lord Richmond described an order to disarm private *592 citizens (not militia members) as "a violation of the constitutional right of Protestant subjects to keep and bear arms for their

---

[14] Faced with this clear historical usage, Justice STEVENS resorts to the bizarre argument that because the word "to" is not included before "bear" (whereas it is included before "petition" in the First Amendment), the unitary meaning of " 'to keep and bear' " is established. *Post*, at 2830, n. 13. We have never heard of the proposition that omitting repetition of the "to" causes two verbs with different meanings to become one. A promise "to support and to defend the Constitution of the United States" is not a whit different from a promise "to support and defend the Constitution of the United States."

own defence." 49 The London Magazine or Gentleman's Monthly Intelligencer 467 (1780). In response, another member of Parliament referred to "the right of bearing arms for personal defence," making clear that no special military meaning for "keep and bear arms" was intended in the discussion. *Id.*, at 467–468.[15]

c. Meaning of the Operative Clause. Putting all of these textual elements together, we find that they guarantee the individual right to possess and carry weapons in case of confrontation. This meaning is strongly confirmed by the historical background of the Second Amendment. We look to this because it has always been widely understood that the Second Amendment, like the First and Fourth Amendments, codified a pre-existing right. The very text of the Second Amendment implicitly recognizes the pre-existence of the right and declares only that it "shall not be infringed." As we said in United States v. Cruikshank, 92 U.S. 542, 553, 23 L.Ed. 588 (1876), "[t]his is not a right granted by the Constitution. Neither is it in any manner dependent upon that instrument for its existence. The second amendment declares that it shall not be infringed ...."[16]

Between the Restoration and the Glorious Revolution, the Stuart Kings Charles II and James II succeeded in using select militias loyal to them to suppress political

---

[15] Cf. 21 Geo. II, ch. 34, § 3, in 7 Eng. Stat. at Large 126 (1748) ("That the Prohibition contained... in this Act, of having, keeping, bearing, or wearing any Arms or Warlike Weapons... shall not extend... to any Officers or their Assistants, employed in the Execution of Justice ...").

[16] Contrary to Justice STEVENS' wholly unsupported assertion, post, at 2831, there was no pre-existing right in English law "to use weapons for certain military purposes" or to use arms in an organized militia.

Putting all of these textual elements together, we find that they guarantee the individual right to possess and carry weapons in case of confrontation.

dissidents, in part by disarming their opponents. See J. Malcolm, To Keep and Bear Arms 31–53 (1994) (hereinafter Malcolm); L. Schwoerer, The Declaration of Rights, 1689, p. 76 (1981). Under the auspices of the 1671 Game Act, for example, the Catholic Charles II had ordered general disarmaments of regions home to his Protestant enemies. See Malcolm 103–106. These experiences caused Englishmen to be extremely wary of concentrated military forces run by the state and to be jealous of their arms. They accordingly obtained an assurance from William and Mary, in the Declaration of Rights (which was codified as the English Bill of Rights), that Protestants would never be disarmed: "That the Subjects which are Protestants, may have Arms for their Defence suitable to their Conditions, and as allowed by Law." 1 W. & M., ch. 2, § 7, in 3 Eng. Stat. at Large 441. This right has long been understood to be the predecessor to our Second Amendment. See E. Dumbauld, The Bill of Rights and What It Means Today 51 (1957); W. Rawle, A View of the Constitution of the United States of America 122 (1825) (hereinafter Rawle). It was clearly an individual right, having nothing whatever to do with service in a militia. To be sure, it was an individual right not available to the whole population, given that it was restricted to Protestants, and like all written English rights it was held only against the Crown, not Parliament. See Schwoerer, To Hold and Bear Arms: The English Perspective, in Bogus 207, 218; but see 3 J. Story, Commentaries on the Constitution of the United States § 1858 (1833) (hereinafter Story) (contending that the "right to bear arms" is a "limitatio[n] upon the power of parliament" as well). But it was secured to them as individuals, according to "libertarian political principles," not as members of a fighting force. Schwoerer, Declaration of Rights, at 283; see also *id.*, at 78; G. Jellinek, The Declaration of the Rights of Man and of Citizens 49, and n. 7 (1901) (reprinted 1979).

By the time of the founding, the right to have arms had become fundamental for English subjects. See Malcolm 122–134. Blackstone, whose works, we have said, "constituted the preeminent authority on English law for the founding generation," *Alden v. Maine*, 527 U.S. 706, 715, 119 S.Ct. 2240, 144 L.Ed.2d 636 (1999), cited the arms provision of the Bill of Rights as one of the fundamental rights of Englishmen. See 1 Blackstone 136, 139–140 (1765). His description of it cannot possibly be thought to tie it to militia or military service. It was, he said, "the natural right of resistance and self-preservation," *id.*, at 139, and "the right of having and using arms for self-preservation and defence," *id.*, at 140; see also 3 *id.*, at 2–4 (1768). Other contemporary authorities concurred. See G. Sharp, Tracts, Concerning the Ancient and Only True Legal Means of National Defence, by a Free Militia 17–18, 27 (3d ed. 1782); 2 J. de Lolme, The Rise and Progress of the English Constitution 886–887 (1784) (A. Stephens ed. 1838); W. Blizard, Desultory Reflections on Police 59–60 (1785). Thus, the right secured in 1689 as a result of the Stuarts' abuses was by

the time of the founding understood to be an individual right protecting against both public and private violence.

And, of course, what the Stuarts had tried to do to their political enemies, George III had tried to do to the colonists. In the tumultuous decades of the 1760's and 1770's, the Crown began to disarm the inhabitants of the most rebellious areas. That provoked polemical reactions by Americans invoking their rights as Englishmen to keep arms. A New York article of April 1769 said that "[i]t is a natural right which the people have reserved to themselves, confirmed by the Bill of Rights, to keep arms for their own defence." A Journal of the Times: Mar. 17, New York Journal, Supp. 1, Apr. 13, 1769, in Boston Under Military Rule 79 (O. Dickerson ed.1936) (reprinted 1970); see also, e.g., Shippen, Boston Gazette, Jan. 30, 1769, in 1 The Writings of Samuel Adams 299 (H. Cushing ed. 1904) (reprinted 1968). They understood the right to enable individuals to defend themselves. As the most important early American edition of Blackstone's Commentaries (by the law professor and former Antifederalist St. George Tucker) made clear in the notes to the description of the arms right, Americans understood the "right of self-preservation" as permitting a citizen to "repe[l] force by force" when "the intervention of society in his behalf, may be too late to prevent an injury." 1 Blackstone's Commentaries 145–146, n. 42 (1803) (hereinafter Tucker's Blackstone). See also W. Duer, Outlines of the Constitutional Jurisprudence of the United States 31–32 (1833).

There seems to us no doubt, on the basis of both text and history, that the Second Amendment conferred an individual right to keep and bear arms. Of course the

There seems to us no doubt, on the basis of both text and history, that the Second Amendment conferred an individual right to keep and bear arms.

right was not unlimited, just as the First Amendment's right of free speech was not, see, *e.g.*, *United States v. Williams*, 553 U.S. 285, 128 S.Ct. 1830, 170 L.Ed.2d 650 (2008). Thus, we do not read the Second Amendment to protect the right of citizens to carry arms for any sort of confrontation, just as we do not read the First Amendment to protect the right of citizens to speak for any purpose. Before turning to limitations upon the individual right, however, we must determine whether the prefatory clause of the Second Amendment comports with our interpretation of the operative clause.

2. Prefatory Clause.

The prefatory clause reads: "A well regulated Militia, being necessary to the security of a free State ...."

a. "Well–Regulated Militia." In *United States v. Miller*, 307 U.S. 174, 179, 59 S.Ct. 816, 83 L.Ed. 1206 (1939), we explained that "the Militia comprised all males physically capable of acting in concert for the common defense." That definition comports with founding-era sources. See, e.g., Webster ("The militia of a country are the able bodied men organized into companies, regiments and brigades... and required by law to attend military exercises on certain days only, but at other times left to pursue their usual occupations"); The Federalist No. 46, pp. 329, 334 (B. Wright ed.1961) (J. Madi-

We do not read the Second Amendment to protect the right of citizens to carry arms for any sort of confrontation, just as we do not read the First Amendment to protect the right of citizens to speak for any purpose.

son) ("near half a million of citizens with arms in their hands"); Letter to Destutt de Tracy (Jan. 26, 1811), in The Portable Thomas Jefferson 520, 524 (M. Peterson ed. 1975) ("the militia of the State, that is to say, of every man in it able to bear arms").

Petitioners take a seemingly narrower view of the militia, stating that "[m]ilitias are the state- and congressionally-regulated military forces described in the Militia Clauses (art. I, § 8, cls. 15–16)." Brief for Petitioners 12. Although we agree with petitioners' interpretive assumption that "militia" means the same thing in Article I and the Second Amendment, we believe that petitioners identify the wrong thing, namely, the organized militia. Unlike armies and navies, which Congress is given the power to create ("to raise... Armies"; "to provide... a Navy," Art. I, § 8, cls. 12–13), the militia is assumed by Article I already to be *in existence*. Congress is given the power to "provide for calling forth the Militia," § 8, cl. 15; and the power not to create, but to "organiz[e]" it—and not to organize "a" militia, which is what one would expect if the militia were to be a federal creation, but to organize "the" militia, connoting a body already in existence, *ibid.*, cl. 16. This is fully consistent with the ordinary definition of the militia as all able-bodied men. From that pool, Congress has plenary power to organize the units that will make up an effective fighting force. That is what Congress did in the first Militia Act, which specified that "each and every free able-bodied white male citizen of the respective states, resident therein, who is or shall be of the age of eighteen years, and under the age of forty-five years (except as is herein after excepted) shall severally and respectively be enrolled in the militia." Act of May 8, 1792, 1 Stat. 271. To be sure, Congress need not conscript every able-bodied man into the militia, because nothing in Article I suggests that in exercising its power to organize, discipline, and arm the militia, Congress must focus upon the entire body. Although the militia consists of all able-bodied men, the federally organized militia may consist of a subset of them.

Finally, the adjective "well-regulated" implies nothing more than the imposition of proper discipline and training. See Johnson 1619 ("Regulate": "To adjust by rule or method"); Rawle 121–122; cf. Va. Declaration of Rights § 13 (1776), in 7 Thorpe 3812, 3814 (referring to "a well-regulated militia, composed of the body of the people, trained to arms").

b. "Security of a Free State." The phrase "security of a free State" meant "security of a free polity," not security of each of the several States as the dissent below argued, see 478 F.3d, at 405, and n. 10. Joseph Story wrote in his treatise on the Constitution that "the word 'state' is used in various senses [and in] its most enlarged sense it means the people composing a particular nation or community." 1 Story § 208; see also 3 id., § 1890 (in reference to the Second Amendment's prefatory clause: "The militia is the natural defence of a free country"). It is true that the term

"State" elsewhere in the Constitution refers to individual States, but the phrase "security of a free State" and close variations seem to have been terms of art in 18th-century political discourse, meaning a " 'free country' " or free polity. See Volokh, "Necessary to the Security of a Free State," 83 Notre Dame L.Rev. 1, 5 (2007); see, *e.g.*, 4 Blackstone 151 (1769); Brutus Essay III (Nov. 15, 1787), in The Essential Antifederalist 251, 253 (W. Allen & G. Lloyd eds., 2d ed.2002). Moreover, the other instances of "state" in the Constitution are typically accompanied by modifiers making clear that the reference is to the several States—"each state," "several states," "any state," "that state," "particular states," "one state," "no state." And the presence of the term "foreign state" in Article I and Article III shows that the word "state" did not have a single meaning in the Constitution.

There are many reasons why the militia was thought to be "necessary to the security of a free State." See 3 Story § 1890. First, of course, it is useful in repelling invasions and suppressing insurrections. Second, it renders large standing armies unnecessary—an argument that Alexander Hamilton made in favor of federal control over the militia. The Federalist No. 29, pp. 226, 227 (B. Wright ed.1961). Third, when the able-bodied men of a nation are trained in arms and organized, they are better able to resist tyranny.

3. Relationship Between Prefatory Clause and Operative Clause.

We reach the question, then: Does the preface fit with an operative clause that creates an individual right to keep and bear arms? It fits perfectly, once one knows the history that the founding generation knew and that we have described above. That history showed that the way tyrants had eliminated a militia consisting of all the able-bodied men was not by banning the militia but simply by taking away the people's arms, enabling a select militia or standing army to suppress political opponents. This is what had occurred in England that prompted codification of the right to have arms in the English Bill of Rights.

The debate with respect to the right to keep and bear arms, as with other guarantees in the Bill of Rights, was not over whether it was desirable (all agreed that it was) but over whether it needed to be codified in the Constitution. During the 1788 ratification debates, the fear that the Federal Government would disarm the people in order to impose rule through a standing army or select militia was pervasive in Antifederalist rhetoric. See, *e.g.*, Letters from The Federal Farmer III (Oct. 10, 1787), in 2 The Complete Anti–Federalist 234, 242 (H. Storing ed.1981). John Smilie, for example, worried not only that Congress's "command of the militia" could be used to create a "select militia," or to have "no militia at all," but also, as a separate concern, that "[w]hen a select militia is formed; the people in general may be disarmed." 2 Documentary History of the Ratification of the Constitution 508–509 (M. Jensen ed.1976) (hereinafter Documentary Hist.). Federalists responded that because Congress was given no power to abridge the ancient right of individuals to keep and bear arms, such a force could never oppress the people. See, *e.g.*, A Pennsylvanian III (Feb. 20, 1788), in The Origin of the Second Amendment 275, 276 (D. Young ed., 2d ed.2001) (hereinafter Young); White, To the Citizens of Virginia (Feb. 22, 1788), in *id.*, at 280, 281; A Citizen of America (Oct. 10, 1787), in *id.*, at 38, 40; Foreign Spectator, Remarks on the Amendments to the Federal Constitution, Nov. 7, 1788, in *id.*, at 556. It was understood across the political spectrum that the right helped to secure the ideal of a citizen militia, which might be necessary to oppose an oppressive military force if the constitutional order broke down.

It is therefore entirely sensible that the Second Amendment's prefatory clause announces the purpose for which the right was codified: to prevent elimination of the militia. The prefatory clause does not suggest that preserving the militia was the only reason Americans valued the ancient right; most undoubtedly thought it even more important for self-defense and hunting. But the threat that the new Federal Government would destroy the citizens' militia by taking away their arms was the reason that right—unlike some other English rights—was codified in a written Constitution. Justice BREYER's assertion that individual self-defense is merely a "subsidiary interest" of the right to keep and bear arms, see *post*, at 2841 (dissenting opinion), is profoundly mistaken. He bases that assertion solely upon the prologue—but that can only show that self-defense had little to do with the right's *codification*; it was the central component of the right itself.

Besides ignoring the historical reality that the Second Amendment was not intended to lay down a "novel principl[e]" but rather codified a right "inherited from our English ancestors," *Robertson v. Baldwin*, 165 U.S. 275, 281, 17 S.Ct. 326, 41 L.Ed. 715 (1897), petitioners' interpretation does not even achieve the narrower purpose that prompted codification of the right. If, as they believe, the Second Amendment right is no more than the right to keep and use weapons as a member of an *organized* militia, see Brief for Petitioners 8—if, that is, the organized militia is the sole institutional beneficiary of the Second Amendment's guarantee—it does not assure the existence of a "citizens' militia" as a safeguard against tyranny. For Congress retains plenary authority to organize the militia, which must include the authority to say who will belong to the organized force.[17] That is why the first Militia Act's requirement that only whites enroll caused States to amend their militia laws to exclude free blacks. See Siegel, The Federal Government's Power to Enact Color–Conscious Laws, 92 Nw. U.L.Rev. 477, 521–525 (1998). Thus, if petitioners are correct, the Second Amendment protects citizens' right to use a gun in an organization from which Congress has

---

[17] Article I, § 8, cl. 16, of the Constitution gives Congress the power

> "[t]o provide for organizing, arming, and disciplining, the Militia, and for governing such Part of them as may be employed in the Service of the United States, reserving to the States respectively, the Appointment of the Officers, and the Authority of training the Militia according to the discipline prescribed by Congress."

It could not be clearer that Congress's "organizing" power, unlike its "governing" power, can be invoked even for that part of the militia not "employed in the Service of the United States." Justice STEVENS provides no support whatever for his contrary view, see *post*, at 2832, n. 20. Both the Federalists and Antifederalists read the provision as it was written, to permit the creation of a "select" militia. See The Federalist No. 29, pp. 226, 227 (B. Wright ed.1961); Centinel, Revived, No. XXIX, Philadelphia Independent Gazetteer, Sept. 9, 1789, in Young 711, 712.

plenary authority to exclude them. It guarantees a select militia of the sort the Stuart kings found useful, but not the people's militia that was the concern of the founding generation.

B

Our interpretation is confirmed by analogous arms-bearing rights in state constitutions that preceded and immediately followed adoption of the Second Amendment. Four States adopted analogues to the Federal Second Amendment in the period between independence and the ratification of the Bill of Rights. Two of them—Pennsylvania and Vermont—clearly adopted individual rights unconnected to militia service. Pennsylvania's Declaration of Rights of 1776 said: "That the people have a right to bear arms *for the defence of themselves* and the state ...." § XIII, in 5 Thorpe 3082, 3083 (emphasis added). In 1777, Vermont adopted the identical provision, except for inconsequential differences in punctuation and capitalization. See Vt. Const., ch. 1, § XV, in 6 *id.*, at 3741.

North Carolina also codified a right to bear arms in 1776: "That the people have a right to bear arms, for the defence of the State ...." Declaration of Rights § XVII, in 5 *id.*, at 2787, 2788. This could plausibly be read to support only a right to bear arms in a militia—but that is a peculiar way to make the point in a constitution that elsewhere repeatedly mentions the militia explicitly. See N. C. Const., §§ XIV, XVIII, XXXV, in *id.*, at 2789, 2791, 2793. Many colonial statutes required individual arms bearing for public-safety reasons—such as the 1770 Georgia law that "for the security and *defence of this prov-*

ince from internal dangers and insurrections" required those men who qualified for militia duty individually "to carry fire arms" "to places of public worship." 19 Colonial Records of the State of Georgia 137–139 (A. Candler ed.1911 (pt. 1)) (emphasis added). That broad public-safety understanding was the connotation given to the North Carolina right by that State's Supreme Court in 1843. See *State v. Huntly*, 25 N.C. 418, 25 N. C. 418, 422–423.

The 1780 Massachusetts Constitution presented another variation on the theme: "The people have a right to keep and to bear arms for the common defence ...." Pt. First, Art. XVII, in 3 Thorpe 1888, 1892. Once again, if one gives narrow meaning to the phrase "common defence" this can be thought to limit the right to the bearing of arms in a state-organized military force. But once again the State's highest court thought otherwise. Writing for the court in an 1825 libel case, Chief Justice Parker wrote: "The liberty of the press was to be unrestrained, but he who used it was to be responsible in cases of its abuse; like the right to keep fire arms, which does not protect him who uses them for annoyance or destruction." *Commonwealth v. Blanding*, 20 Mass. 304, 313–314. The analogy makes no sense if firearms could not be used for any individual purpose at all. See also Kates, Handgun Prohibition and the Original Meaning of the Second Amendment, 82 Mich. L.Rev. 204, 244 (1983) (19th-century courts never read "common defence" to limit the use of weapons to militia service).

We therefore believe that the most likely reading of all four of these pre-Second Amendment state constitutional provisions is that they secured an individual right to bear arms for defensive purposes. Other States did not include rights to bear arms in their pre–1789 constitutions—although in Virginia a Second Amendment analogue was proposed (unsuccessfully) by Thomas Jefferson. (It read: "No freeman shall ever be debarred the use of arms [within his own lands or tenements]."[18] 1 The Papers of Thomas Jefferson 344 (J. Boyd ed. 1950).)

Between 1789 and 1820, nine States adopted Second Amendment analogues. Four of them—Kentucky, Ohio, Indiana, and Missouri—referred to the right of the people to "bear arms in defence of themselves and the State." See n. 8, *supra*. Another three States—Mississippi, Connecticut, and Alabama—used the even more individualistic phrasing that each citizen has the "right to bear arms in defence of himself and the State." See *ibid.* Finally, two States—Tennessee and Maine—used the "common defence" language of Massachusetts. See Tenn. Const., Art. XI, § 26 (1796), in 6 Thorpe 3414, 3424; Me. Const., Art. I, § 16 (1819), in 3 *id.*, at 1646, 1648. That of the nine state constitutional protections for the right to bear arms enacted immediately after 1789 at least seven unequivocally protected an individual citizen's right to self-defense is strong evidence that that is how the founding generation conceived of the right. And with one possible exception that we discuss in Part II–D–2, 19th-century courts and commentators interpreted these state constitutional provisions to pro-

---

[18] Justice STEVENS says that the drafters of the Virginia Declaration of Rights rejected this proposal and adopted "instead" a provision written by George Mason stressing the importance of the militia. See *post*, at 2835, and n. 24. There is no evidence that the drafters regarded the Mason proposal as a substitute for the Jefferson proposal.

tect an individual right to use arms for self-defense. See n. 9, *supra*; *Simpson v. State*, 13 Tenn. 356, 5 Yer. 356, 360 (1833).

The historical narrative that petitioners must endorse would thus treat the Federal Second Amendment as an odd outlier, protecting a right unknown in state constitutions or at English common law, based on little more than an overreading of the prefatory clause.

C

Justice STEVENS relies on the drafting history of the Second Amendment—the various proposals in the state conventions and the debates in Congress. It is dubious to rely on such history to interpret a text that was widely understood to codify a pre-existing right, rather than to fashion a new one. But even assuming that this legislative history is relevant, Justice STEVENS flatly misreads the historical record.

It is true, as Justice STEVENS says, that there was concern that the Federal Government would abolish the institution of the state militia. See *post*, at 2832–2833. That concern found expression, however, *not* in the various Second Amendment precursors proposed in the state conventions, but in separate structural provisions that would have given the States concurrent and seemingly non-preemptible authority to organize, discipline, and arm the militia when the Federal Government failed to do so. See Veit 17, 20 (Virginia proposal); 4 J. Eliot, The Debates in the Several State Conventions on the Adoption of the Federal Constitution 244, 245 (2d ed. 1836) (reprinted 1941) (North Carolina proposal); see also 2 Documentary Hist. 624 (Pennsylvania minority's proposal). The Second Amendment precursors, by contrast, referred to the individual English right already codified in two (and probably four) state constitutions. The Federalist-dominated first Congress chose to reject virtually all major structural revisions favored by the Antifederalists, including the proposed militia amendments. Rather, it adopted primarily the popular and uncontroversial (though, in the Federalists' view, unnecessary) individual-rights amendments. The Second Amendment right, protecting only individuals' liberty to keep and carry arms, did nothing to assuage Antifederalists' concerns about federal control of the militia. See, *e.g.*, Centinel, Revived, No. XXIX, Philadelphia Independent Gazetteer, Sept. 9, 1789, in Young 711, 712.

Justice STEVENS thinks it significant that the Virginia, New York, and North Carolina Second Amendment proposals were "embedded ... within a group of principles that are distinctly military in meaning," such as statements about the danger of standing armies. *Post*, at 2833 – 2834. But so was the highly influential minority proposal in Pennsylvania, yet that proposal, with its reference to hunting, plainly referred to an individual right. See 2 Documentary Hist. 624. Other than that erroneous point, Justice STEVENS has brought forward absolutely no evidence that those proposals conferred only a right to carry arms in a militia. By contrast, New Hampshire's proposal, the Pennsylvania minority's proposal, and Samuel Adams' proposal in Massachusetts unequivocally referred to individual rights, as did two state constitutional provisions at the time. See Veit 16, 17 (New Hampshire proposal); 6 Documentary Hist. 1452, 1453 (J. Kaminski & G. Saladino eds. 2000)

(Samuel Adams' proposal). Justice STEVENS' view thus relies on the proposition, unsupported by any evidence, that different people of the founding period had vastly different conceptions of the right to keep and bear arms. That simply does not comport with our longstanding view that the Bill of Rights codified venerable, widely understood liberties.

D

We now address how the Second Amendment was interpreted from immediately after its ratification through the end of the 19th century. Before proceeding, however, we take issue with Justice STEVENS' equating of these sources with postenactment legislative history, a comparison that betrays a fundamental misunderstanding of a court's interpretive task. See *post*, at 2837, n. 28. " '[L]egislative history,' " of course, refers to the pre-enactment statements of those who drafted or voted for a law; it is considered persuasive by some, not because they reflect the general understanding of the disputed terms, but because the legislators who heard or read those statements presumably voted with that understanding. *Ibid.* "[P]ostenactment legislative history," *ibid.*, a deprecatory contradiction in terms, refers to statements of those who drafted or voted for the law that are made after its enactment and hence could have had no effect on the congressional vote. It most certainly does not refer to the examination of a variety of legal and other sources to determine *the public understanding* of a legal text in the period after its enactment or ratification. That sort of inquiry is a critical tool of constitutional interpretation. As we will show, virtually all interpreters of the Second

Amendment in the century after its enactment interpreted the Amendment as we do.

1. Postratification Commentary.

Three important founding-era legal scholars interpreted the Second Amendment in published writings. All three understood it to protect an individual right unconnected with militia service.

St. George Tucker's version of Blackstone's Commentaries, as we explained above, conceived of the Blackstonian arms right as necessary for self-defense. He equated that right, absent the religious and class-based restrictions, with the Second Amendment. See 2 Tucker's Blackstone 143. In Note D, entitled, "View of the Constitution of the United States," Tucker elaborated on the Second Amendment: "This may be considered as the true palladium of liberty ... The right to self defence is the first law of nature: in most governments it has been the study of rulers to confine the right within the narrowest limits possible. Wherever standing armies are kept up, and the right of the people to keep and bear arms is, under any colour or pretext whatsoever, prohibited, liberty, if not already annihilated, is on the brink of destruction." 1 *id.*, at App. 300 (ellipsis in original). He believed that the English game laws had abridged the right by prohibiting "keeping a gun or other engine for the destruction of game." *Ibid.*; see also 2 *id.*, at 143, and nn. 40 and 41. He later grouped the right with some of the individual rights included in the First Amendment and said that if "a law be passed by congress, prohibiting" any of those rights, it would "be the province of the judiciary to pronounce whether any such act were constitutional, or not;

and if not, to acquit the accused ...." 1 *id.*, at App. 357.
It is unlikely that Tucker was referring to a person's being
"accused" of violating a law making it a crime to bear
arms in a state militia.[19]

In 1825, William Rawle, a prominent lawyer who
had been a member of the Pennsylvania Assembly that
ratified the Bill of Rights, published an influential treatise, which analyzed the Second Amendment as follows:

> "The first [principle] is a declaration that a
> well regulated militia is necessary to the secu-
> rity of a free state; a proposition from which
> few will dissent ....
>
> "The corollary, from the first position is, that
> the right of the people to keep and bear arms
> shall not be infringed.
>
> "The prohibition is general. No clause in the
> constitution could by any rule of construc-
> tion be conceived to give to congress a power
> to disarm the people. Such a flagitious at-
> tempt could only be made under some gen-
> eral pretence by a state legislature. But if in
> any blind pursuit of inordinate power, either
> should attempt it, this amendment may be

---

[19] Justice Stevens quotes some of Tucker's unpublished notes, which
he claims show that Tucker had ambiguous views about the Second
Amendment. See *post*, at 31, and n. 32. But it is clear from the notes
that Tucker located the power of States to arm their militias in the
Tenth Amendment, and that he cited the Second Amendment for the
proposition that such armament could not run afoul of any power of
the Federal Government (since the Amendment prohibits Congress
from ordering disarmament). Nothing in the passage implies that the
Second Amendment pertains only to the carrying of arms in the organized militia.

appealed to as a restraint on both." Rawle 121–122.[20]

Like Tucker, Rawle regarded the English game laws as violating the right codified in the Second Amendment. See *id.*, at 122–123. Rawle clearly differentiated between the people's right to bear arms and their service in a militia: "In a people permitted and accustomed to bear arms, we have the rudiments of a militia, which properly consists of armed citizens, divided into military bands, and instructed at least in part, in the use of arms for the purposes of war." *Id.*, at 140. Rawle further said that the Second Amendment right ought not "be abused to the disturbance of the public peace," such as by assembling with other armed individuals "for an unlawful purpose"—statements that make no sense if the right does not extend to any individual purpose. *Id.*, at 123.

Joseph Story published his famous Commentaries on the Constitution of the United States in 1833. Justice STEVENS suggests that "[t]here is not so much as a whisper" in Story's explanation of the Second Amendment that favors the individual-rights view. *Post*, at 2840. That is wrong. Story explained that the English Bill of Rights had also included a "right to bear arms," a right that, as we have discussed, had nothing to do with militia service. 3 Story § 1858. He then equated the English right with the Second Amendment:

---

20 Rawle, writing before our decision in *Barron ex rel. Tiernan v. Mayor of Baltimore*, 7 Pet. 243, 8 L.Ed. 672 (1833), believed that the Second Amendment could be applied against the States. Such a belief would of course be nonsensical on petitioners' view that it protected only a right to possess and carry arms when conscripted by the State itself into militia service.

"§ 1891. A similar provision [to the Second Amendment] in favour of protestants (for to them it is confined) is to be found in the bill of rights of 1688, it being declared, 'that the subjects, which are protestants, may have arms for their defence suitable to their condition, and as allowed by law.' But under various pretences the effect of this provision has been greatly narrowed; and it is at present in England more nominal than real, as a defensive privilege." (Footnotes omitted.)

This comparison to the Declaration of Right would not make sense if the Second Amendment right was the right to use a gun in a militia, which was plainly not what the English right protected. As the Tennessee Supreme Court recognized 38 years after Story wrote his Commentaries, "[t]he passage from Story, shows clearly that this right was intended... and was guaranteed to, and to be exercised and enjoyed by the citizen as such, and not by him as a soldier, or in defense solely of his political rights." *Andrews v. State*, 50 Tenn. 165, 183–184 (1871). Story's Commentaries also cite as support Tucker and Rawle, both of whom clearly viewed the right as unconnected to militia service. See 3 Story § 1890, n. 2, § 1891, n. 3. In addition, in a shorter 1840 work Story wrote: "One of the ordinary modes, by which tyrants accomplish their purposes without resistance, is, by disarming the people, and making it an offence to keep arms, and by substituting a regular army in the stead of a resort to the militia." A Familiar Exposition of the Constitution of the United States § 450 (reprinted 1986).

Antislavery advocates routinely invoked the right to bear arms for self-defense. Joel Tiffany, for example, citing Blackstone's description of the right, wrote that "the right to keep and bear arms, also implies the right to use them if necessary in self defence; without this right to use the guaranty would have hardly been worth the paper it consumed." A Treatise on the Unconstitutionality of American Slavery 117–118 (1849); see also L. Spooner, The Unconstitutionality of Slavery 116 (1845) (right enables "personal defence"). In his famous Senate speech about the 1856 "Bleeding Kansas" conflict, Charles Sumner proclaimed:

> "The rifle has ever been the companion of the pioneer and, under God, his tutelary protector against the red man and the beast of the forest. Never was this efficient weapon more needed in just self-defense, than now in Kansas, and at least one article in our National Constitution must be blotted out, before the complete right to it can in any way be impeached. And yet such is the madness of the hour, that, in defiance of the solemn guarantee, embodied in the Amendments to the Constitution, that 'the right of the people to keep and bear arms shall not be infringed,' the people of Kansas have been arraigned for keeping and bearing them, and the Senator from South Carolina has had the face to say openly, on this floor, that they should be disarmed—of course, that the fanatics of Slavery, his allies and constituents, may meet no

impediment." The Crime Against Kansas, May 19–20, 1856, in American Speeches: Political Oratory From the Revolution to the Civil War 553, 606–607 (T. Widmer ed. 2006).

We have found only one early-19th century-commentator who clearly conditioned the right to keep and bear arms upon service in the militia—and he recognized that the prevailing view was to the contrary. "The provision of the constitution, declaring the right of the people to keep and bear arms, & c. was probably intended to apply to the right of the people to bear arms for such [militia-related] purposes only, and not to prevent congress or the legislatures of the different states from enacting laws to prevent the citizens from always going armed. A different construction however has been given to it." B. Oliver, The Rights of an American Citizen 177 (1832).

2. Pre–Civil War Case Law.

The 19th-century cases that interpreted the Second Amendment universally support an individual right unconnected to militia service. In *Houston v. Moore,* 5 Wheat. 1, 24, 5 L.Ed. 19 (1820), this Court held that States have concurrent power over the militia, at least where not pre-empted by Congress. Agreeing in dissent that States could "organize, arm, and discipline" the militia in the absence of conflicting federal regulation, Justice Story said that the Second Amendment "may not, perhaps, be thought to have any important bearing on this point. If it have, it confirms and illustrates, rather than impugns the reasoning already suggested." *Id.*, at 51–53. Of course, if the Amendment simply "protect[ed] the right of the people of each of the several States to maintain a well-regulated militia," post, at 2822 (STEVENS, J., dissenting), it would have enormous and obvious bearing on the point. But the Court and Story derived the States' power over the militia from the non-exclusive nature of federal power, not from the Second Amendment, whose preamble merely "confirms and illustrates" the importance of the militia. Even clearer was Justice Baldwin. In the famous fugitive-slave case of *Johnson v. Tompkins*, 13 F. Cas. 840, 850, 852 (CC Pa. 1833), Baldwin, sitting as a Circuit Judge, cited both the Second Amendment and the Pennsylvania analogue for his conclusion that a citizen has "a right to carry arms in defence of his property or person, and to use them, if either were assailed with such force, numbers or violence as made it necessary for the protection or safety of either."

Many early-19th century state cases indicated that the Second Amendment right to bear arms was an individual right unconnected to militia service, though subject to certain restrictions. A Virginia case in 1824 holding that the Constitution did not extend to free blacks explained: "[N]umerous restrictions imposed on [blacks] in our Statute Book, many of which are inconsistent with the letter and spirit of the Constitution, both of this State and of the United States as respects the free whites, demonstrate, that, here, those instruments have not been considered to extend equally to both classes of our population. We will only instance the restriction upon the migration of free blacks into this State, and upon their right to bear arms." *Aldridge v. Commonwealth*, 4 Va. 447, 2 Va. Cas. 447, 449 (Gen.Ct.). The claim was obviously not that blacks were prevented from carrying guns in the militia.[21] See also *Waters v. State*, 1 Gill 302, 309 (Md.1843) (because free blacks were treated as a "dangerous population," "laws have been passed to prevent their migration into this State; to make it unlawful for them to bear arms; to guard even their religious assemblages with peculiar watchfulness"). An 1829 decision by the Supreme Court of Michigan said: "The constitution of the United States also grants to the citizen the right to keep and bear arms. But the grant of this privilege cannot be construed into the right in him who keeps a gun to destroy his neighbor. No rights are intended to be granted by the constitution for an unlawful or unjustifiable purpose." *United States v. Sheldon*, in 5 Transactions of the Supreme Court of the Territory of Michigan 337, 346 (W. Blume ed.1940) (hereinafter Blume). It is not

---

[21] Justice STEVENS suggests that this is not obvious because free blacks in Virginia had been required to muster without arms. See *post*, at 2837, n. 29 (citing Siegel, The Federal Government's Power to Enact Color–Conscious Laws, 92 Nw. U.L.Rev. 477, 497 (1998)). But that could not have been the type of law referred to in *Aldridge,* because that practice had stopped 30 years earlier when blacks were excluded entirely from the militia by the first militia Act. See Siegel, *supra,* at 498, n. 120. Justice STEVENS further suggests that laws barring blacks from militia service could have been said to violate the "right to bear arms." But under Justice STEVENS' reading of the Second Amendment (we think), the protected right is the right to carry arms to the extent one is enrolled in the militia, not the right *to be in the militia*. Perhaps Justice STEVENS really does adopt the full-blown idiomatic meaning of "bear arms," in which case every man and woman in this country has a right "to be a soldier" or even "to wage war." In any case, it is clear to us that *Aldridge's* allusion to the existing Virginia "restriction" upon the right of free blacks "to bear arms" could only have referred to "laws prohibiting free blacks from keeping weapons," Siegel, *supra,* at 497–498.

possible to read this as discussing anything other than an individual right unconnected to militia service. If it did have to do with militia service, the limitation upon it would not be any "unlawful or unjustifiable purpose," but any nonmilitary purpose whatsoever.

In *Nunn v. State*, 1 Ga. 243, 251 (1846), the Georgia Supreme Court construed the Second Amendment as protecting the "*natural* right of self-defence" and therefore struck down a ban on carrying pistols openly. Its opinion perfectly captured the way in which the operative clause of the Second Amendment furthers the purpose announced in the prefatory clause, in continuity with the English right:

> "The right of the whole people, old and young, men, women and boys, and not militia only, to keep and bear *arms* of every description, and not *such* merely as are used by the *militia*, shall not be *infringed*, curtailed, or broken in upon, in the smallest degree; and all this for the important end to be attained: the rearing up and qualifying a well-regulated militia, so vitally necessary to the security of a free State. Our opinion is, that any law, State or Federal, is repugnant to the Constitution, and void, which contravenes this *right*, originally belonging to our forefathers, trampled under foot by Charles I. and his two wicked sons and successors, re-established by the revolution of 1688, conveyed to this land of liberty by the colonists, and fi-

nally incorporated conspicuously in our own *Magna Charta!*" *Ibid.*

Likewise, in *State v. Chandler,* 5 La. Ann. 489, 490 (1850), the Louisiana Supreme Court held that citizens had a right to carry arms openly: "This is the right guaranteed by the Constitution of the United States, and which is calculated to incite men to a manly and noble defence of themselves, if necessary, and of their country, without any tendency to secret advantages and unmanly assassinations."

Those who believe that the Second Amendment preserves only a militia-centered right place great reliance on the Tennessee Supreme Court's 1840 decision in *Aymette v. State,* 21 Tenn. 154. The case does not stand for that broad proposition; in fact, the case does not mention the word "militia" at all, except in its quoting of the Second Amendment. *Aymette* held that the state constitutional guarantee of the right to "bear" arms did not prohibit the banning of concealed weapons. The opinion first recognized that both the state right and the federal right were descendents of the 1689 English right, but (erroneously, and contrary to virtually all other authorities) read that right to refer only to "protect[ion of] the public liberty" and "keep[ing] in awe those who are in power," *id.,* at 158. The court then adopted a sort of middle position, whereby citizens were permitted to carry arms openly, unconnected with any service in a formal militia, but were given the right to use them only for the military purpose of banding together to oppose tyranny. This odd reading of the right is, to be sure, not the one we adopt—but it is not petitioners' reading either. More importantly, seven years earlier the Tennessee Supreme Court had treated the state constitutional provision as conferring a right "to all the free citizens of the State to keep and bear arms for their defence," *Simpson*, 13 Tenn. 356, 5 Yer., at 360; and 21 years later the court held that the "keep" portion of the state constitutional right included the right to personal self-defense: "[T]he right to keep arms involves, necessarily, the right to use such arms for all the ordinary purposes, and in all the ordinary modes usual in the country, and to which arms are adapted, limited by the duties of a good citizen in times of peace." *Andrews*, 50 Tenn., at 178–179; see also *ibid.* (equating state provision with Second Amendment).

3. Post–Civil War Legislation.

In the aftermath of the Civil War, there was an outpouring of discussion of the Second Amendment in Congress and in public discourse, as people debated whether and how to secure constitutional rights for newly free slaves. See generally S. Halbrook, Freedmen, the Fourteenth Amendment, and the Right to Bear Arms, 1866–1876 (1998) (hereinafter Halbrook); Brief for Institute for Justice as *Amicus Curiae*. Since those discussions took place 75 years after the ratification of the Second Amendment, they do not provide as much insight into its original meaning as earlier sources. Yet those born and educated in the early 19th century faced a widespread effort to limit arms ownership by a large number of citizens; their understanding of the origins and continuing significance of the Amendment is instructive.

Blacks were routinely disarmed by Southern States after the Civil War. Those who opposed these injustices frequently stated that they infringed blacks' constitutional right to keep and bear arms. Needless to say, the claim was not that blacks were being prohibited from carrying arms in an organized state militia. A Report of the Commission of the Freedmen's Bureau in 1866 stated plainly: "[T]he civil law [of Kentucky] prohibits the colored man from bearing arms... Their arms are taken from them by the civil authorities... Thus, the right of the people to keep and bear arms as provided in the Constitution is *infringed*." H.R. Exec. Doc. No. 70, 39th Cong., 1st Sess., 233, 236. A joint congressional Report decried:

> "[I]n some parts of [South Carolina,] armed parties are, without proper authority, engaged in seizing all fire-arms found in the hands of the freedmen. Such conduct is in plain and direct violation of their personal rights as guaranteed by the Constitution of the United States, which declares that 'the right of the people to keep and bear arms shall not be infringed.' The freedmen of South Carolina have shown by their peaceful and orderly conduct that they can safely be trusted with fire-arms, and they need them to kill game for subsistence, and to protect their crops from destruction by birds and animals." Joint Comm. on Reconstruction, H.R.Rep. No. 30, 39th Cong., 1st Sess., pt. 2, p. 229 (1866) (Proposed Circular of Brigadier General R. Saxton).

The view expressed in these statements was widely reported and was apparently widely held. For example, an editorial in The Loyal Georgian (Augusta) on February 3, 1866, assured blacks that "[a]ll men, without distinction of color, have the right to keep and bear arms to defend their homes, families or themselves." Halbrook 19.

Congress enacted the Freedmen's Bureau Act on July 16, 1866. Section 14 stated:

> "[T]he right... to have full and equal benefit of all laws and proceedings concerning personal liberty, personal security, and the acquisition, enjoyment, and disposition of estate, real and personal, including the constitutional right to bear arms, shall be secured to and enjoyed by all the citizens... without respect to race or color, or previous condition of slavery ...." 14 Stat. 176–177.

The understanding that the Second Amendment gave freed blacks the right to keep and bear arms was reflected in congressional discussion of the bill, with even an opponent of it saying that the founding generation "were for every man bearing his arms about him and keeping them in his house, his castle, for his own defense." Cong. Globe, 39th Cong., 1st Sess., 362, 371 (1866) (Sen. Davis).

Similar discussion attended the passage of the Civil Rights Act of 1871 and the Fourteenth Amendment. For example, Representative Butler said of the Act: "Section eight is intended to enforce the well-known constitutional provision guaranteeing the right of the citizen to 'keep and bear arms,' and provides that whoever shall take away, by force or violence, or by threats and intimidation, the arms and weapons which any person may have for his defense, shall be deemed guilty of larceny of the same." H.R.Rep. No. 37, 41st Cong., 3d Sess., 7–8 (1871). With respect to the proposed Amendment, Senator Pomeroy described as one of the three "indispensable" "safeguards of liberty... under the Constitution" a man's "right to bear arms for the defense of himself and family and his homestead." Cong. Globe, 39th Cong., 1st Sess., 1182 (1866). Representative Nye thought the Fourteenth Amendment unnecessary because "[a]s citizens of the United States [blacks] have equal right to protection, and to keep and bear arms for self-defense." *Id.*, at 1073.

It was plainly the understanding in the post-Civil War Congress that the Second Amendment protected an individual right to use arms for self-defense.

4. Post–Civil War Commentators.

Every late–19th–century legal scholar that we have read interpreted the Second Amendment to secure an individual right unconnected with militia service. The most famous was the judge and professor Thomas Cooley, who wrote a massively popular 1868 Treatise on Constitutional Limitations. Concerning the Second Amendment it said:

> "Among the other defences to personal liberty should be mentioned the right of the people to keep and bear arms... The alternative to a standing army is 'a well-regulated militia,' but this cannot exist unless the people are trained to bearing arms. How far it is

It was plainly the understanding in the post-Civil War Congress that the Second Amendment protected an individual right to use arms for self-defense.

in the power of the legislature to regulate this right, we shall not undertake to say, as happily there has been very little occasion to discuss that subject by the courts." *Id.*, at 350.

That Cooley understood the right not as connected to militia service, but as securing the militia by ensuring a populace familiar with arms, is made even clearer in his 1880 work, General Principles of Constitutional Law. The Second Amendment, he said, "was adopted with some modification and enlargement from the English Bill of Rights of 1688, where it stood as a protest against arbitrary action of the overturned dynasty in disarming the people." *Id.*, at 270. In a section entitled "The Right in General," he continued:

"It might be supposed from the phraseology of this provision that the right to keep and bear arms was only guaranteed to the militia; but this would be an interpretation not warranted by the intent. The militia, as has been elsewhere explained, consists of those persons who, under the law, are liable to the performance of military duty, and are officered and enrolled for service when called upon. But the law may make provision for the enrolment of all who are fit to perform military duty, or of a small number only, or it may wholly omit to make any provision at all; and if the right were limited to those enrolled, the purpose of this guaranty might be defeated altogether by the action or neglect to act of the government it was meant to hold in check. The meaning of the provision undoubtedly is, that the people, from whom the militia must be taken, shall have the right to keep and bear arms; and they need no permission or regulation of law for the purpose. But this enables government to have a well-regulated militia; for to bear arms implies something more than the mere keeping; it implies the learning to handle and use them in a way that makes those who keep them ready for their efficient use; in other words, it implies the right to meet for voluntary discipline in arms, observing in doing so the laws of public order." *Id.*, at 271.

All other post-Civil War 19th-century sources we have found concurred with Cooley. One example from each decade will convey the general flavor:

"[The purpose of the Second Amendment is] to secure a well-armed militia... But a militia would be useless unless the citizens were enabled to exercise themselves in the use of warlike weapons. To preserve this privilege, and to secure to the people the ability to oppose themselves in military force against the usurpations of government, as well as against enemies from without, that government is

[The purpose of the Second Amendment is] to secure a well-armed militia… But a militia would be useless unless the citizens were enabled to exercise themselves in the use of warlike weapons. To preserve this privilege, and to secure to the people the ability to oppose themselves in military force against the usurpations of government, as well as against enemies from without, that government is forbidden by any law or proceeding to invade or destroy the right to keep and bear arms.

forbidden by any law or proceeding to invade or destroy the right to keep and bear arms… The clause is analogous to the one securing the freedom of speech and of the press. Freedom, not license, is secured; the fair use, not the libellous abuse, is protected." J. Pomeroy, An Introduction to the Constitutional Law of the United States § 239, pp. 152–153 (1868) (hereinafter Pomeroy).

"As the Constitution of the United States, and the constitutions of several of the states, in terms more or less comprehensive, declare the right of the people to keep and bear arms, it has been a subject of grave discussion, in some of the state courts, whether a statute prohibiting persons, when not on a journey, or as travellers, from *wearing or carrying concealed weapons*, be constitutional. There has been a great difference of opinion on the question." 2 J. Kent, Commentaries on American Law *340, n. 2 (O. Holmes ed., 12th ed. 1873) (hereinafter Kent).

"Some general knowledge of firearms is important to the public welfare; because it would be impossible, in case of war, to organize promptly an efficient force of volunteers unless the people had some familiarity with weapons of war. The Constitution secures the right of the people to keep and bear arms. No doubt, a citizen who keeps a gun or pistol under judicious precautions, practises in safe places the use of it, and in due time teaches his sons to do the same, exercises his individual right. No doubt, a person whose residence or duties involve peculiar peril may keep a pistol for prudent self-defence." B. Abbott, Judge and Jury: A Popular Explanation of the Leading Topics in the Law of the Land 333 (1880) (hereinafter Abbott).

"The right to bear arms has always been the distinctive privilege of freemen. Aside from any necessity of self-protection to the person, it represents among all nations power coupled with the exercise of a certain jurisdiction. ... [I]t was not necessary that the right to bear arms should be granted in the Constitution, for it had always existed." J. Ordronaux, Constitutional Legislation in the United States 241–242 (1891).

E

We now ask whether any of our precedents forecloses the conclusions we have reached about the meaning of the Second Amendment.

United States v. Cruikshank, 92 U.S. 542, 23 L.Ed. 588, in the course of vacating the convictions of members of a white mob for depriving blacks of their right to keep and bear arms, held that the Second Amendment does not by its own force apply to anyone other than the Federal Government. The opinion explained that the right "is not a right granted by the Constitution [or] in any manner dependent upon that instrument for its existence. The second amendment... means no more than that it shall not be infringed by Congress." *Id.*, at 553. States, we said, were free to restrict or protect the right under their police powers. The limited discussion of the Second Amendment in *Cruikshank* supports, if anything, the individual-rights interpretation. There was no claim in *Cruikshank* that the victims had been deprived of their right to carry arms in a militia; indeed, the Governor had disbanded the local militia unit the year before the mob's attack, see C. Lane, The Day Freedom Died 62 (2008). We described the right protected by the Second Amendment as "'bearing arms for a lawful purpose'"[22] and said that "the people [must] look for their protection against any violation by their fellow-citizens of the rights it recognizes" to the States' police power. 92 U.S., at 553.

---

[22] Justice STEVENS' accusation that this is "not accurate," *post*, at 2843, is wrong. It is true it was the indictment that described the right as "bearing arms for a lawful purpose." But, in explicit reference to the right described in the indictment, the Court stated that "[t]he second amendment declares that it [*i.e.*, the right of bearing arms for a lawful purpose] shall not be infringed." 92 U.S., at 553.

That discussion makes little sense if it is only a right to bear arms in a state militia.[23]

Presser v. Illinois, 116 U.S. 252, 6 S.Ct. 580, 29 L.Ed. 615 (1886), held that the right to keep and bear arms was not violated by a law that forbade "bodies of men to associate together as military organizations, or to drill or parade with arms in cities and towns unless authorized by law." *Id.*, at 264–265, 6 S.Ct. 580. This does not refute the individual-rights interpretation of the Amendment; no one supporting that interpretation has contended that States may not ban such groups. Justice STEVENS presses *Presser* into service to support his view that the right to bear arms is limited to service in the militia by joining *Presser's* brief discussion of the Second Amendment with a later portion of the opinion making the seemingly relevant (to the Second Amendment) point that the plaintiff was not a member of the state militia. Unfortunately for Justice STEVENS' argument, that later portion deals with the *Fourteenth Amendment*; it was the *Fourteenth Amendment* to which the plaintiff's nonmembership in the militia was relevant. Thus, Justice STEVENS' statement that *Presser* "suggested that ... nothing in the Constitution protected the use of arms outside the context of a militia," *post*, at 2843, is simply wrong. *Presser* said nothing about the Second Amend-

---

[23] With respect to *Cruikshank's* continuing validity on incorporation, a question not presented by this case, we note that *Cruikshank* also said that the First Amendment did not apply against the States and did not engage in the sort of Fourteenth Amendment inquiry required by our later cases. Our later decisions in *Presser v. Illinois*, 116 U.S. 252, 265, 6 S.Ct. 580, 29 L.Ed. 615 (1886), and *Miller v. Texas,* 153 U.S. 535, 538, 14 S.Ct. 874, 38 L.Ed. 812 (1894), reaffirmed that the Second Amendment applies only to the Federal Government.

ment's meaning or scope, beyond the fact that it does not prevent the prohibition of private paramilitary organizations.

Justice STEVENS places overwhelming reliance upon this Court's decision in *Miller,* 307 U.S. 174, 59 S.Ct. 816, 83 L.Ed. 1206. "[H]undreds of judges," we are told, "have relied on the view of the Amendment we endorsed there," *post*, at 2823, and "[e]ven if the textual and historical arguments on both sides of the issue were evenly balanced, respect for the well-settled views of all of our predecessors on this Court, and for the rule of law itself... would prevent most jurists from endorsing such a dramatic upheaval in the law," *post*, at 2824. And what is, according to Justice STEVENS, the holding of *Miller* that demands such obeisance? That the Second Amendment "protects the right to keep and bear arms for certain military purposes, but that it does not curtail the Legislature's power to regulate the nonmilitary use and ownership of weapons." *Post*, at 2823.

Nothing so clearly demonstrates the weakness of Justice STEVENS' case. *Miller* did not hold that and cannot possibly be read to have held that. The judgment in the case upheld against a Second Amendment challenge two men's federal indictment for transporting an unregistered short-barreled shotgun in interstate commerce, in violation of the National Firearms Act, 48 Stat. 1236. It is entirely clear that the Court's basis for saying that the Second Amendment did not apply was *not* that the defendants were "bear [ing] arms" not "for... military purposes" but for "nonmilitary use," *post*, at 2823. Rather, it was that the *type of weapon at issue* was not eligible for Second Amendment protection: "In the absence of any evidence tending to show that the pos-session or use of a [short-barreled shotgun] at this time has some reasonable relationship to the preservation or efficiency of a well regulated militia, we cannot say that the Second Amendment guarantees the right to keep and bear *such an instrument*." 307 U.S., at 178, 59 S.Ct. 816 (emphasis added). "Certainly," the Court continued, "it is not within judicial notice that this weapon is any part of the ordinary military equipment or that its use could contribute to the common defense." *Ibid.* Beyond that, the opinion provided no explanation of the content of the right.

This holding is not only consistent with, but posi-tively suggests, that the Second Amendment confers an individual right to keep and bear arms (though only arms that "have some reasonable relationship to the preservation or efficiency of a well regulated militia"). Had the Court believed that the Second Amendment protects only those serving in the militia, it would have been odd to examine the character of the weapon rather than simply note that the two crooks were not militia-men. Justice STEVENS can say again and again that *Miller* did not "turn on the difference between muskets and sawed-off shotguns; it turned, rather, on the basic difference between the military and nonmilitary use and possession of guns," *post*, at 2845, but the words of the opinion prove otherwise. The most Justice STEVENS can plausibly claim for *Miller* is that it declined to decide the nature of the Second Amendment right, despite the Solicitor General's argument (made in the alternative) that the right was collective, see Brief for United States, O.T.1938, No. 696, pp. 4–5. *Miller* stands only for the proposition that the Second Amendment right, whatever its nature, extends only to certain types of weapons.

It is particularly wrongheaded to read *Miller* for more than what it said, because the case did not even purport to be a thorough examination of the Second Amendment. Justice STEVENS claims, *post*, at 2845, that the opinion reached its conclusion "[a]fter reviewing many of the same sources that are discussed at greater length by the Court today." Not many, which was not entirely the Court's fault. The defendants made no appearance in the case, neither filing a brief nor appearing at oral argument; the Court heard from no one but the Government (reason enough, one would think, not to make that case the beginning and the end of this Court's consideration of the Second Amendment). See Frye, The Peculiar Story of *United States v. Miller*, 3 N.Y.U.J.L. & Liberty 48, 65–68 (2008). The Government's brief spent two pages discussing English legal sources, concluding "that at least the carrying of weapons without lawful occasion or excuse was always a crime" and that (because of the class-based restrictions and the prohibition on terrorizing people with dangerous or unusual weapons) "the early English law did not guarantee an unrestricted right to bear arms." Brief for United States, O.T.1938, No. 696, at 9–11. It then went on to rely primarily on the discussion of the English right to bear arms in *Aymette v. State*, 21 Tenn. 154, for the proposition that the only uses of arms protected by the Second Amendment are those that relate to the militia, not self-defense. See Brief for United States, O.T.1938, No. 696, at 12–18. The final section of the brief recognized that "some courts have said that the right to bear arms includes the right of the individual to have them for the protection of his person and property," and launched an alternative argument that "weapons which are commonly used by criminals," such as sawed-off shotguns, are not protected. See *id.*, at 18–21. The Government's *Miller* brief thus provided scant discussion of the history of the Second Amendment—and the Court was presented with no counterdiscussion. As for the text of the Court's opinion itself, that discusses *none* of the history of the Second Amendment. It assumes from the prologue that the Amendment was designed to preserve the militia, 307 U.S., at 178, 59 S.Ct. 816 (which we do not dispute), and then reviews some historical materials dealing with the nature of the militia, and in particular with the nature of the arms their members were expected to possess, *id.*, at 178–182, 59 S.Ct. 816. Not a word (*not a word*) about the history of the Second Amendment. This is the mighty rock upon which the dissent rests its case.[24]

We may as well consider at this point (for we will have to consider eventually) *what* types of weapons *Miller* permits. Read in isolation, *Miller's* phrase "part of ordinary military equipment" could mean that only those weapons useful in warfare are protected. That would be a startling reading of the opinion, since it would mean

---

[24] As for the "hundreds of judges," *post*, at 2823, who have relied on the view of the Second Amendment Justice STEVENS claims we endorsed in *Miller*. If so, they overread *Miller*. And their erroneous reliance upon an uncontested and virtually unreasoned case cannot nullify the reliance of millions of Americans (as our historical analysis has shown) upon the true meaning of the right to keep and bear arms. In any event, it should not be thought that the cases decided by these judges would necessarily have come out differently under a proper interpretation of the right.

that the National Firearms Act's restrictions on machine-guns (not challenged in *Miller*) might be unconstitutional, machineguns being useful in warfare in 1939. We think that *Miller 's* "ordinary military equipment" language must be read in tandem with what comes after: "[O]rdinarily when called for [militia] service [able-bodied] men were expected to appear bearing arms supplied by themselves and of the kind in common use at the time." 307 U.S., at 179, 59 S.Ct. 816. The traditional militia was formed from a pool of men bringing arms "in common use at the time" for lawful purposes like self-defense. "In the colonial and revolutionary war era, [small-arms] weapons used by militiamen and weapons used in defense of person and home were one and the same." *State v. Kessler*, 289 Ore. 359, 368, 614 P.2d 94, 98 (1980) (citing G. Neumann, Swords and Blades of the American Revolution 6–15, 252–254 (1973)). Indeed, that is precisely the way in which the Second Amendment's operative clause furthers the purpose announced in its preface. We therefore read *Miller* to say only that the Second Amendment does not protect those weapons not typically possessed by law-abiding citizens for lawful purposes, such as short-barreled shotguns. That accords with the historical understanding of the scope of the right, see Part III, *infra*.[25]

---

[25] Miller was briefly mentioned in our decision in *Lewis v. United States*, 445 U.S. 55, 100 S.Ct. 915, 63 L.Ed.2d 198 (1980), an appeal from a conviction for being a felon in possession of a firearm. The challenge was based on the contention that the prior felony conviction had been unconstitutional. No Second Amendment claim was raised or briefed by any party. In the course of rejecting the asserted challenge, the Court commented gratuitously, in a footnote, that "[t]hese legislative restrictions on the use of firearms are neither based upon

> *We therefore read* Miller *to say only that the Second Amendment does not protect those weapons not typically possessed by law-abiding citizens for lawful purposes, such as short-barreled shotguns.*

We conclude that nothing in our precedents forecloses our adoption of the original understanding of the Second Amendment. It should be unsurprising that such a significant matter has been for so long judicially unresolved. For most of our history, the Bill of Rights was not thought applicable to the States, and the Federal Government did not significantly regulate the possession of firearms by law-abiding citizens. Other provisions of the Bill of Rights have similarly remained unilluminated for lengthy periods. This Court first held a law to violate the First Amendment's guarantee of freedom of speech in 1931, almost 150 years after the Amendment was ratified, see *Near v. Minnesota ex rel. Olson*, 283 U.S. 697, 51 S.Ct. 625, 75 L.Ed. 1357 (1931), and it was not until after World War II that we held a law invalid under the Establishment Clause, see *Illinois ex rel. McCollum v. Board of Ed. of School Dist. No. 71, Champaign Cty.*, 333 U.S. 203, 68 S.Ct. 461, 92 L.Ed. 649 (1948). Even a question as basic as the scope of proscribable li-

---

constitutionally suspect criteria, nor do they trench upon any constitutionally protected liberties. See *United States v. Miller*… (the Second Amendment guarantees no right to keep and bear a firearm that does not have 'some reasonable relationship to the preservation or efficiency of a well regulated militia')." *Id.*, at 65–66, n. 8, 100 S.Ct. 915. The footnote then cites several Court of Appeals cases to the same effect. It is inconceivable that we would rest our interpretation of the basic meaning of any guarantee of the Bill of Rights upon such a footnoted dictum in a case where the point was not at issue and was not argued.

bel was not addressed by this Court until 1964, nearly two centuries after the founding. See N*ew York Times Co. v. Sullivan*, 376 U.S. 254, 84 S.Ct. 710, 11 L.Ed.2d 686 (1964). It is demonstrably not true that, as Justice STEVENS claims, *post*, at 2844–2845, "for most of our history, the invalidity of Second–Amendment–based objections to firearms regulations has been well settled and uncontroversial." For most of our history the question did not present itself.

III

Like most rights, the right secured by the Second Amendment is not unlimited. From Blackstone through the 19th-century cases, commentators and courts routinely explained that the right was not a right to keep and carry any weapon whatsoever in any manner whatsoever and for whatever purpose. See, *e.g.*, *Sheldon*, in 5 Blume 346; Rawle 123; Pomeroy 152–153; Abbott 333. For example, the majority of the 19th-century courts to consider the question held that prohibitions on carrying concealed weapons were lawful under the Second Amendment or state analogues. See, *e.g.*, *State v. Chandler*, 5 La. Ann., at 489–490; *Nunn v. State*, 1 Ga., at 251; see generally 2 Kent *340, n. 2; The American Students' Blackstone 84, n. 11 (G. Chase ed. 1884). Although we do not undertake an exhaustive historical analysis today of the full scope of the Second Amend-

---

Like most rights, the right secured by the Second Amendment is not unlimited.

The right was not a right to keep and carry any weapon whatsoever in any manner whatsoever and for whatever purpose.

ment, nothing in our opinion should be taken to cast doubt on longstanding prohibitions on the possession of firearms by felons and the mentally ill, or laws forbidding the carrying of firearms in sensitive places such as schools and government buildings, or laws imposing conditions and qualifications on the commercial sale of arms.[26]

We also recognize another important limitation on the right to keep and carry arms. *Miller* said, as we have explained, that the sorts of weapons protected were those "in common use at the time." 307 U.S., at 179, 59 S.Ct. 816. We think that limitation is fairly supported by the historical tradition of prohibiting the carrying of "dangerous and unusual weapons." See 4 Blackstone 148–149 (1769); 3 B. Wilson, Works of the Honourable James Wilson 79 (1804); J. Dunlap, The New–York Justice 8 (1815); C. Humphreys, A Compendium of the Common Law in Force in Kentucky 482 (1822); 1 W. Russell, A Treatise on Crimes and Indictable Misdemeanors 271–272 (1831); H. Stephen, Summary of the Criminal Law 48 (1840); E. Lewis, An Abridgment of the Criminal Law of the United States 64 (1847); F. Wharton, A Treatise on the Criminal Law of the United States 726 (1852). See also *State v. Langford*, 10 N.C.

---

[26] We identify these presumptively lawful regulatory measures only as examples; our list does not purport to be exhaustive.

Although we do not undertake an exhaustive historical analysis today of the full scope of the Second Amendment, nothing in our opinion should be taken to cast doubt on longstanding prohibitions on the possession of firearms by felons and the mentally ill, or laws forbidding the carrying of firearms in sensitive places such as schools and government buildings, or laws imposing conditions and qualifications on the commercial sale of arms.

381, 383–384 (1824); *O'Neill v. State*, 16 Ala. 65, 67 (1849); *English v. State*, 35 Tex. 473, 476 (1871); *State v. Lanier*, 71 N.C. 288, 289 (1874).

It may be objected that if weapons that are most useful in military service—M–16 rifles and the like—may be banned, then the Second Amendment right is completely detached from the prefatory clause. But as we have said, the conception of the militia at the time of the Second Amendment's ratification was the body of all citizens capable of military service, who would bring the sorts of lawful weapons that they possessed at home to militia duty. It may well be true today that a militia, to be as effective as militias in the 18th century, would require sophisticated arms that are highly unusual in society at large. Indeed, it may be true that no amount of small arms could be useful against modern-day bombers and tanks. But the fact that modern developments have limited the degree of fit between the prefatory clause and the protected right cannot change our interpretation of the right.

---

*We also recognize another important limitation
on the right to keep and carry arms...
the sorts of weapons protected were those
"in common use at the time."*

IV

We turn finally to the law at issue here. As we have said, the law totally bans handgun possession in the home. It also requires that any lawful firearm in the home be disassembled or bound by a trigger lock at all times, rendering it inoperable.

As the quotations earlier in this opinion demonstrate, the inherent right of self-defense has been central to the Second Amendment right. The handgun ban amounts to a prohibition of an entire class of "arms" that is overwhelmingly chosen by American society for that lawful purpose. The prohibition extends, moreover, to the home, where the need for defense of self, family, and property is most acute. Under any of the standards of scrutiny that we have applied to enumerated constitutional rights,[27] banning from the home "the most pre-

---

[27] Justice BREYER correctly notes that this law, like almost all laws, would pass rational-basis scrutiny. *Post*, at 2850–2851. But rational-basis scrutiny is a mode of analysis we have used when evaluating laws under constitutional commands that are themselves prohibitions on irrational laws. See, *e.g.*, *Engquist v. Oregon Dept. of Agriculture*, 553 U.S. 591, 602, 128 S.Ct. 2146, 2153–2154, 2008 WL 2329768, *6–7, 170 L.Ed.2d 975 (2008). In those cases, "rational basis" is not just the standard of scrutiny, but the very substance of the constitutional guarantee. Obviously, the same test could not be used to evaluate the extent to which a legislature may regulate a specific, enumerated right, be it the freedom of speech, the guarantee against double jeopardy, the right to counsel, or the right to keep and bear arms. See *United States*

The handgun ban amounts to a prohibition of an entire class of "arms" that is overwhelmingly chosen by American society for that lawful purpose.

ferred firearm in the nation to 'keep' and use for protection of one's home and family," 478 F.3d, at 400, would fail constitutional muster.

Few laws in the history of our Nation have come close to the severe restriction of the District's handgun ban. And some of those few have been struck down. In *Nunn v. State*, the Georgia Supreme Court struck down a prohibition on carrying pistols openly (even though it upheld a prohibition on carrying concealed weapons). See 1 Ga., at 251. In *Andrews v. State*, the Tennessee Supreme Court likewise held that a statute that forbade openly carrying a pistol "publicly or privately, without regard to time or place, or circumstances," 50 Tenn., at 187, violated the state constitutional provision (which the court equated with the Second Amendment). That was so even though the statute did not restrict the carrying of long guns. *Ibid.* See also *State v. Reid*, 1 Ala. 612, 616–617 (1840) ("A statute which, under the pretence of regulating, amounts to a destruction of the right, or which requires arms to be so borne as to render them

---

v. Carolene Products Co., 304 U.S. 144, 152, n. 4, 58 S.Ct. 778, 82 L.Ed. 1234 (1938) ("There may be narrower scope for operation of the presumption of constitutionality [i.e., narrower than that provided by rational-basis review] when legislation appears on its face to be within a specific prohibition of the Constitution, such as those of the first ten amendments ..."). If all that was required to overcome the right to keep and bear arms was a rational basis, the Second Amendment would be redundant with the separate constitutional prohibitions on irrational laws, and would have no effect.

> *Under any of the standards of scrutiny that we have applied to enumerated constitutional rights, banning from the home "the most preferred firearm in the nation to 'keep' and use for protection of one's home and family," would fail constitutional muster.*

wholly useless for the purpose of defence, would be clearly unconstitutional").

It is no answer to say, as petitioners do, that it is permissible to ban the possession of handguns so long as the possession of other firearms (*i.e.*, long guns) is allowed. It is enough to note, as we have observed, that the American people have considered the handgun to be the quintessential self-defense weapon. There are many reasons that a citizen may prefer a handgun for home defense: It is easier to store in a location that is readily accessible in an emergency; it cannot easily be redirected or wrestled away by an attacker; it is easier to use for those without the upper-body strength to lift and aim a long gun; it can be pointed at a burglar with one hand while the other hand dials the police. Whatever the reason, handguns are the most popular weapon chosen by Americans for self-defense in the home, and a complete prohibition of their use is invalid.

We must also address the District's requirement (as applied to respondent's handgun) that firearms in the home be rendered and kept inoperable at all times. This makes it impossible for citizens to use them for the core lawful purpose of self-defense and is hence unconstitutional. The District argues that we should interpret this element of the statute to contain an exception for self-de-

*It is no answer to say that it is permissible to
ban the possession of handguns so long as the
possession of other firearms is allowed.*

fense. See Brief for Petitioners 56–57. But we think that
is precluded by the unequivocal text, and by the presence
of certain other enumerated exceptions: "Except for law
enforcement personnel..., each registrant shall keep any
firearm in his possession unloaded and disassembled or
bound by a trigger lock or similar device unless such firearm is kept at his place of business, or while being used
for lawful recreational purposes within the District of
Columbia." D.C.Code § 7–2507.02. The nonexistence
of a self-defense exception is also suggested by the D.C.
Court of Appeals' statement that the statute forbids residents to use firearms to stop intruders, see *McIntosh v.
Washington*, 395 A.2d 744, 755–756 (1978).[28]

Apart from his challenge to the handgun ban and the
trigger-lock requirement respondent asked the District
Court to enjoin petitioners from enforcing the separate
licensing requirement "in such a manner as to forbid the
carrying of a firearm within one's home or possessed land
without a license." App. 59a. The Court of Appeals did
not invalidate the licensing requirement, but held only
that the District "may not prevent [a handgun] from be-

---

[28] *McIntosh* upheld the law against a claim that it violated the Equal
Protection Clause by arbitrarily distinguishing between residences
and businesses. See 395 A.2d, at 755. One of the rational bases listed
for that distinction was the legislative finding "that for each intruder
stopped by a firearm there are four gun-related accidents within the
home." *Ibid.* That tradeoff would not bear mention if the statute did
not prevent stopping intruders by firearms.

Whatever the reason, handguns are the most popular weapon chosen by Americans for self-defense in the home, and a complete prohibition of their use is invalid.

ing moved throughout one's house." 478 F.3d, at 400. It then ordered the District Court to enter summary judgment "consistent with [respondent's] prayer for relief." *Id.*, at 401. Before this Court petitioners have stated that "if the handgun ban is struck down and respondent registers a handgun, he could obtain a license, assuming he is not otherwise disqualified," by which they apparently mean if he is not a felon and is not insane. Brief for Petitioners 58. Respondent conceded at oral argument that he does not "have a problem with... licensing" and that the District's law is permissible so long as it is "not enforced in an arbitrary and capricious manner." Tr. of Oral Arg. 74–75. We therefore assume that petitioners' issuance of a license will satisfy respondent's prayer for relief and do not address the licensing requirement.

Justice BREYER has devoted most of his separate dissent to the handgun ban. He says that, even assuming the Second Amendment is a personal guarantee of the right to bear arms, the District's prohibition is valid. He first tries to establish this by founding-era historical precedent, pointing to various restrictive laws in the colonial period. These demonstrate, in his view, that the District's law "imposes a burden upon gun owners that seems proportionately no greater than restrictions in existence at the time the Second Amendment was adopted." *Post*, at 2848. Of the laws he cites, only one offers even marginal support for his assertion. A 1783 Massachusetts law forbade the residents of Boston to "take into" or "receive into" "any Dwelling-House, Stable, Barn, Out-house, Ware-house, Store, Shop or other Building" loaded firearms, and permitted the seizure of any loaded firearms that "shall be found" there. Act of Mar. 1, 1783, ch. XIII, 1783 Mass. Acts p. 218. That statute's text and its prologue, which makes clear that the purpose of the prohibition was to eliminate the danger to firefighters posed by the "depositing of loaded Arms" in buildings, give reason to doubt that colonial Boston authorities would have enforced that general prohibition against someone who temporarily loaded a firearm to confront an intruder (despite the law's application in that case). In any case, we would not stake our interpretation of the Second Amendment upon a single law, in effect in a single city, that contradicts the overwhelming weight of other evidence regarding the right to keep and bear arms for defense of the home. The other laws Justice BREYER cites are gunpowder-storage laws that he concedes did not clearly prohibit loaded weapons, but required only that excess gunpowder be kept in a special container or on the top floor of the home. *Post*, at 2849–2850. Nothing about those fire-safety laws undermines our analysis; they do not remotely burden the right of self-defense as much as an absolute ban on handguns. Nor, correspondingly, does our analysis suggest the invalidity of laws regulating the storage of firearms to prevent accidents.

Justice BREYER points to other founding-era laws that he says "restricted the firing of guns within the city limits to at least some degree" in Boston, Philadelphia,

Nor, correspondingly, does our analysis suggest the invalidity of laws regulating the storage of firearms to prevent accidents.

and New York. *Post*, at 2848 (citing Churchill, Gun Regulation, the Police Power, and the Right to Keep Arms in Early America, 25 Law & Hist. Rev. 139, 162 (2007)). Those laws provide no support for the severe restriction in the present case. The New York law levied a fine of 20 shillings on anyone who fired a gun in certain places (including houses) on New Year's Eve and the first two days of January, and was aimed at preventing the "great Damages... frequently done on [those days] by persons going House to House, with Guns and other Fire Arms and being often intoxicated with Liquor." Ch. 1501, 5 Colonial Laws of New York 244–246 (1894). It is inconceivable that this law would have been enforced against a person exercising his right to self-defense on New Year's Day against such drunken hooligans. The Pennsylvania law to which Justice BREYER refers levied a fine of five shillings on one who fired a gun or set off fireworks in Philadelphia without first obtaining a license from the Governor. See Act of Aug. 26, 1721, ch. CCXLV, § IV, in 3 Stat. at Large of Pa. 253–254 (1896). Given Justice Wilson's explanation that the right to self-defense with arms was protected by the Pennsylvania Constitution, it is unlikely that this law (which in any event amounted to at most a licensing regime) would have been enforced against a person who used firearms for self-defense. Justice BREYER cites a Rhode Island law that simply levied a 5–shilling fine on those who fired guns in *streets* and *taverns*, a law obviously inapplicable to this case. See An Act for preventing Mischief being done in the town of *Newport*, or in any other Town in this Government, 1731 Rhode Island Session Laws, pp. 240–241. Finally, Justice BREYER points to a Massachusetts law similar to the Pennsylvania law, prohibiting "discharg[ing] any Gun or Pistol charged with Shot or Ball in the Town of *Boston*." Act of May 28, 1746, ch. X, Acts and Laws of Mass. Bay p. 208. It is again implausible that this would have been enforced against a citizen acting in self-defense, particularly given its preambulatory reference to "the *indiscreet* firing of Guns." *Ibid.* (preamble) (emphasis added).

A broader point about the laws that Justice BREYER cites: All of them punished the discharge (or loading) of guns with a small fine and forfeiture of the weapon (or in a few cases a very brief stay in the local jail), not with significant criminal penalties.[29] They are akin to modern penalties for minor public-safety infractions like speeding or jaywalking. And although such public-safety laws may not contain exceptions for self-defense, it is inconceivable that the threat of a jaywalking ticket would deter someone from disregarding a "Do Not Walk" sign in order to flee an attacker, or that the government would enforce those laws under such circumstances. Likewise, we do not think that a law imposing a 5–shilling fine and forfeiture of the gun would have prevented a person in the founding era from using a gun to protect himself

---

[29] The Supreme Court of Pennsylvania described the amount of five shillings in a contract matter in 1792 as "nominal consideration." *Morris's Lessee v. Smith*, 4 Dall. 119, 120, 1 L.Ed. 766 (Pa.1792). Many of the laws cited punished violation with fine in a similar amount; the 1783 Massachusetts gunpowder-storage law carried a somewhat larger fine of £ 10 (200 shillings) and forfeiture of the weapon.

or his family from violence, or that if he did so the law would be enforced against him. The District law, by contrast, far from imposing a minor fine, threatens citizens with a year in prison (five years for a second violation) for even obtaining a gun in the first place. See D.C.Code § 7–2507.06.

Justice BREYER moves on to make a broad jurisprudential point: He criticizes us for declining to establish a level of scrutiny for evaluating Second Amendment restrictions. He proposes, explicitly at least, none of the traditionally expressed levels (strict scrutiny, intermediate scrutiny, rational basis), but rather a judge-empowering "interest-balancing inquiry" that "asks whether the statute burdens a protected interest in a way or to an extent that is out of proportion to the statute's salutary effects upon other important governmental interests." *Post*, at 2852. After an exhaustive discussion of the arguments for and against gun control, Justice BREYER arrives at his interest-balanced answer: Because handgun violence is a problem, because the law is limited to an urban area, and because there were somewhat similar restrictions in the founding period (a false proposition that we have already discussed), the interest-balancing inquiry results in the constitutionality of the handgun ban. QED.

We know of no other enumerated constitutional right whose core protection has been subjected to a

---

...this case represents this Court's first in-depth examination of the Second Amendment, one should not expect it to clarify the entire field...

freestanding "interest-balancing" approach. The very enumeration of the right takes out of the hands of government—even the Third Branch of Government—the power to decide on a case-by-case basis whether the right is *really worth* insisting upon. A constitutional guarantee subject to future judges' assessments of its usefulness is no constitutional guarantee at all. Constitutional rights are enshrined with the scope they were understood to have when the people adopted them, whether or not future legislatures or (yes) even future judges think that scope too broad. We would not apply an "interest-balancing" approach to the prohibition of a peaceful neo-Nazi march through Skokie. See *National Socialist Party of America v. Skokie*, 432 U.S. 43, 97 S.Ct. 2205, 53 L.Ed.2d 96 (1977) (*per curiam*). The First Amendment contains the freedom-of-speech guarantee that the people ratified, which included exceptions for obscenity, libel, and disclosure of state secrets, but not for the expression of extremely unpopular and wrong headed views. The Second Amendment is no different. Like the First, it is the very *product* of an interest balancing by the people—which Justice BREYER would now conduct for them anew. And whatever else it leaves to future evaluation, it surely elevates above all other interests the right

In sum, we hold that the District's ban on handgun possession in the home violates the Second Amendment, as does its prohibition against rendering any lawful firearm in the home operable for the purpose of immediate self-defense.

But the enshrinement of constitutional rights
necessarily takes certain policy choices off the table.
These include the absolute prohibition of handguns
held and used for self-defense in the home.

---

of law-abiding, responsible citizens to use arms in defense of hearth and home.

Justice BREYER chides us for leaving so many applications of the right to keep and bear arms in doubt, and for not providing extensive historical justification for those regulations of the right that we describe as permissible. See *post*, at 2869–2870. But since this case represents this Court's first in-depth examination of the Second Amendment, one should not expect it to clarify the entire field, any more than *Reynolds v. United States*, 98 U.S. 145, 25 L.Ed. 244 (1879), our first in-depth Free Exercise Clause case, left that area in a state of utter certainty. And there will be time enough to expound upon the historical justifications for the exceptions we have mentioned if and when those exceptions come before us.

In sum, we hold that the District's ban on handgun possession in the home violates the Second Amendment, as does its prohibition against rendering any lawful firearm in the home operable for the purpose of immediate self-defense. Assuming that Heller is not disqualified from the exercise of Second Amendment rights, the District must permit him to register his handgun and must issue him a license to carry it in the home.

* * *

> *... what is not debatable is that it is not*
> *the role of this Court to pronounce the*
> *Second Amendment extinct.*

We are aware of the problem of handgun violence in this country, and we take seriously the concerns raised by the many *amici* who believe that prohibition of handgun ownership is a solution. The Constitution leaves the District of Columbia a variety of tools for combating that problem, including some measures regulating handguns, see *supra*, at 2816–2817, and n. 26. But the enshrinement of constitutional rights necessarily takes certain policy choices off the table. These include the absolute prohibition of handguns held and used for self-defense in the home. Undoubtedly some think that the Second Amendment is outmoded in a society where our standing army is the pride of our Nation, where well-trained police forces provide personal security, and where gun violence is a serious problem. That is perhaps debatable, but what is not debatable is that it is not the role of this Court to pronounce the Second Amendment extinct.

We affirm the judgment of the Court of Appeals.

It is so ordered.

MICHEL & ASSOCIATES, P.C.
Attorneys at Law

Helping Firearms Owners, Businesses, Ranges and Clubs Nationwide

FIREARMS | ENVIRONMENTAL | LAND USE | CIVIL RIGHTS ADVOCACY
LABOR & EMPLOYMENT | CIVIL LITIGATION | CRIMINAL DEFENSE

LEGAL *FIREPOWER*

- Civil Litigation
- Restoration of Gun Rights
- Gun Seizures & Returns
- Inventory Cataloging
- Restraining Order Removal
- Criminal Defense
- Hunter & Hunting Protection
- Regulatory Compliance Checks
- Governmental Licensing & Permits
- Range Protection & Development
- Range Environmental Issues
- Explosives & Destructive Devices
- Entertainment Industry Props
  & Much More

Michel & Associates, P.C.
180 East Ocean Boulevard, Suite 200
Long Beach, California 90802
(562) 216-4444
www.MichelLawyers.com

Free Gun Law Info
www.CalGunLaws.com

Michel & Associates, P.C., is a full-service law firm representing businesses throughout the country. Owner C.D. "Chuck" Michel leads a team of over a dozen highly qualified and experienced attorneys with extensive experience in a variety of legal specialties. The firm has been litigating civil and criminal firearm cases since 1991.

Some law firms undermine your right to keep and bear arms by providing *pro bono* legal services to politicians who would deprive you of your Second Amendment rights. This *pro bono* work is subsidized through the legal fees paid by business clients. Since it was formed, **Michel & Associates has provided over $3 million worth of *pro bono* legal service to indigent gun owners, and to the non-profit associations that protect your rights.** Shop for your legal service provider carefully so you don't inadvertently subsidize the gun ban lobby!

As attorneys for the NRA, CRPA, firearm manufacturers, wholesalers, retailers, and firearms owners the lawyers at Michel & Associates have litigated thousands of cases involving civil rights issues, including Second Amendment challenges, in both state and federal trial and appellate courts. They have represented clients in high-profile cases that have garnered national media attention and have appeared as spokespersons for the NRA and CRPA.

Mr. Michel is frequently quoted concerning Second Amendment rights by the major daily newspapers and by television and radio stations. He is the author of *California Gun Laws: A Guide to State and Federal Firearm Regulations* (available at www.CalGunLawsBook.com.) Mr. Michel has been honored and profiled in recognition of his corporate and civil rights work in multiple periodicals and by the NRA, which awarded him the prestigious *Defender of Justice* Award in 2013. Mr. Michel also teaches *Firearms Law* and *Law Practice Management* at Chapman University Dale E. Fowler School of Law.

MORE LAWYERS | MORE EXPERIENCE | MORE RELATIONSHIPS | MORE RESOURCES | MORE RESULTS

Coming Soon from:

California Gun Laws: A Guide to State and Federal Firearm Regulations (2020 7th ed.)

Freedom Week

Gun Truths: A Compilation of Research & Empirical Studies Proving that Gun Control Laws Fail

Gun Owner's Guide to Police Encounters: Know All Your Constitutional Rights & Avoid Becoming an Accidental Criminal